THE MUSIC MEN

THE GUYS WHO SANG WITH THE BANDS AND BEYOND

by

RICHARD GRUDENS

Author of *The Best Damn Trumpet Player*

and *The Song Stars*

CELEBRITY PROFILES PUBLISHING

Stony Brook, New York 11790-0344

516-862-8555

CANDID PHOTOS BY

WILLIAM DE BETTA, C. CAMILLE SMITH AND GUS YOUNG.

Library of Congress
Catalog Card Number 98-71248

ISBN 1-57579-097-1

Published by:
Celebrity Profiles Publishing Inc.
Box 344, Main Street
Stony Brook, New York 11790-0344
(516) 862-8555
Fax (516) 862-0139

Edited by MaryLou Facciola

Printed in United States of America

PINE HILL PRESS, INC.
Freeman, S. Dak. 57029

Bob Hope and Richard Grudens meet once again to talk about *The Music Men*. **(photo by C. Camille Smith)**

INTRODUCTION AND ACKNOWLEDGMENTS

by Richard Grudens

It's been two years since I first introduced *The Best Damn Trumpet Player*, and one year since *The Song Stars*.

Among the comments and suggestions sent to me regarding *The Song Stars* there arose a stirring interest in portraying the biographies of the men vocalists to compliment the ladies of *The Song Stars*. Kitty Kallen first suggested: "How about a sequel about the guys (singers). I'll be happy to help. Call me!" Connie Haines seconded the motion. Rosemary Clooney said: "A sequel about the boys—yes—of course, and don't forget my friend Bing." Jack Rael, Patti Page's manager and partner for over 50 years, concurred emphatically, as did vocalist Lynn Roberts. Frances Langford responded: "Great idea, and don't forget Matt Munroe." Big Band vocalist experts, critic and writer Anthony De Florio III of Philadelphia; Jack Ellsworth of WLIM and Chris Valenti of WHPC on Long Island; Al "Jazzbeaux" Collins of KCSM, San Mateo, California; Joe Pardee of the The Harry James Appreciation Society, Frank Esposito of *Remember When Magazine,* and Mike Prelee of WVNJ in New Jersey also urged me on, all recommending coverage of their favorite vocalists. Max Wirz of Big Band radio Thurgau in Switzerland became very excited about the prospect of a book about the men vocalists and sent in his contribution featuring the Europeans.

As the project idea moved forward, my friend and mentor Frankie Laine and I held a meeting of the minds, if you will. We talked about some of the male singers he knew and worked with over the years. I would submit a name, and Frank would impart his take. Frank is much revered and respected in the industry, so his input was invaluable.

I approached Lee Hale, whose song *The Ladies Who Sang With the Bands* was featured in *The Song Stars*, to write about Dean Martin whom he knew intimately, having been his musical director and stand-in for all of Dean's television shows. We even sought out comedian Dom De Luise for his take on Dean, and he was also eager to contribute.

Lovely Kathryn Crosby cheerfully reviewed the chapter about her beloved Bing and his inspiration, Al Jolson, and composed an interesting letter about an unknown Crosby singing secret that for the first time will be revealed. Helen Forrest, between hospital stays (the last for pneumonia), talked to me at length about her friend and co-star Dick Haymes. Don Kennedy of Big Band Jump in Atlanta, who pronounces Dick and Helen to be the best voices of the era, furnished additional data and some great photos.

Maria (Ellington) Cole and I shared several conversations and exchanged letters about her wonderful husband Nat King Cole. The chapter featuring Nat, considered and reviewed by her, would have been diminished without her bountiful contribution. Young Sam Arlen and I sat in his living room viewing videos, listening to tapes, and culling through photos about his "singer" father, prolific song writer Harold Arlen.

Marvelous Tess—Tess Russell of The Society of Singers became the real catalyst of *The Music Men*. Tess diligently researched the whereabouts of many of the men singers whom I was unable to locate. Tess knows them all, having once been the long time artists relations director for famous Hollywood disc jockey Whit Whittinghill. Tess and I talked, faxed, wrote, finally locating a lot of those guys who sang with the bands, and even some who didn't. It would have been a much less interesting book without her willing and dedicated assistance.

Tess also recommended a chapter about the arrangers, promptly furnishing the whereabouts of three of the greatest, Billy May, Frank De Vol, and Pete Rugolo. It's in here, too!

Music Men is the chronicle of the thrilling male voices of our lifetime. It is an important story each participant was anxious to express to you, reader and fan.

Additionally, I must acknowledge a host of friends and helpers, especially MaryLou Facciola, my editor and literary advisor; Anthony

DiFlorio III for his all-around advice and ideas; my wife Jeanette for her down-to-earth words of counterbalance and perspective; Don Kennedy of *Big Band Jump* for his continual commitment to the cause; Dan Kellachan of Westbury Music Fair for his assistance; author George Simon for those veritable observations in his book *The Big Bands* and *Glenn Miller;* Bandleader Red Norvo for his help with Frank Sinatra; Connie Haines for her consistent, infectious enthusiasm; author and broadcaster Fred Hall for his contributions; photographers C. Camille Smith, Bill DeBetta, and Gus Young; Iris Cornell for help with hubby Don Cornell; Mitch Miller for more than can ever be acknowledged; Robert Scott for his assistance with Johnny Mathis, and Roger Dooner for his knowledgeable guidance with respect to Dick Haymes. A special thanks to publicist Ward Grant for his assistance with the greatest living entertainer Bob Hope.

Last, but certainly not least, thanks to all the singers, and I mean all the singers who ever graced a bandstand or faced a microphone. I hope I included all of them.

So here for your distinct pleasure and reminiscence is *The Music Men.*

I know Bing is smiling.

Richard Grudens,
Stony Brook, New York
January 1998

L to R: A young Steve Lawrence, PFC Eddie Fisher, DJ Brad Phillips, Al Martino and Dick Haymes at a reception for Radio Station WINS (in New York) *Singing Battle Royal.* (Roger Dooner, Dick Haymes Society Collection)

FOREWORD

Those Wonderful Guys
by Bob Hope

Well, it's been just about sixty-four years, and it went pretty fast, I wanna tell you. Even though everyone knows I left England when I was four because I found out I could never be king, I still managed to get started in a Jerome Kern Broadway musical in 1933, called *Roberta*. I played a character named Huckleberry Haines, no relation to Connie. Then I moved to Hollywood where I warbled my favorite, bittersweet tune *Thanks For the Memory* with Shirley Ross in a movie called *The Big Broadcast of 1938*. I haven't let go of that song since.

Looking back, those vaudeville and big band days were really something. I was kind of lucky working alongside many young male vocalists who worked very hard to establish themselves, trying to build their careers with the bands working vaudeville stages, and on radio and television shows. One of them was a guy called Bing Crosby. Funny name, Bing. I told him he'd never make it.

During the Second World War (You remember World War II—it was in all the papers), and later in Korea and Vietnam, I had the privilege of working with some of those great guys, and later with fellows like Bill Farrell at Weisbaden, Germany, 1948, Andy Williams at Guantanamo Bay, Cuba, in 1960, Jack Jones at Tan Son Nhut, Vietnam, 1965, Vic Damone at Chu Lai, Vietnam, 1966, Eddie Fisher at Bienhoa, Vietnam, in 1967, and then that guy called Bing I was telling you about, who finally learned to sing under my tutelage in all those Road pictures, and finally made the big-time.

Richard Grudens has honored all of them, right here. Jolson and Crosby. Sinatra and Bennett. Como and Cornell. Tony Martin and Dean Martin. Joe Williams and Andy Williams. Jeffries and Vale. Damone and Lawrence. Fisher and Beneke. Mathis and Martino. La Rosa and

Tormé. Maria Cole tells Nat's story, Lee Hale tells Dean's story. Dom De Luise also tells about Dean (How did a comedian get in here?). Lovely songbird Helen Forrest tells Dick Haymes' story, and Kathryn helped out with Bing.

There is also a chapter on all the early vocalists. Who could forget Rudy Vallee, Ted Lewis, Jack Teagarden, Cab Calloway, Fats Waller, Phil Harris, and Arthur Tracy, the Street Singer? I knew them all.

And the arrangers are here too: Gordon Jenkins, Don Costa, Nelson Riddle, George Siravo, and Billy May. We all traveled the same road, like ships passing in the night.

All the great ones and the not so great ones are also here, all of them in one terrific book, *The Music Men.* So grab an hour and check out this tribute. As Buddy Rich once said to author Richard Grudens during an interview: "It's not a step back—this is not nostalgia—this is music to my ears."

Gotta go now, I'm still working on my first Oscar. Thanks for the memory.

Bob Hope, Hollywood, California January, 1998.

TABLE OF CONTENTS

PART ONE:

PART TWO:

PART THREE:

**The many faces of Kathryn Crosby's best friend.
(Richard Grudens Collection)**

A TRIBUTE TO AL JOLSON AND BING CROSBY

AL JOLSON—The foundation. "You ain't heard nothin' yet, Bing!"
BING CROSBY—The builder. "Just call me lucky, Al. I love to sing, but if I had style, it was composed of my imitating you on my dad's old phonograph records."

It is accepted in the world of music and elsewhere that prolific crooner Bing Crosby was the very first Big Band male vocalist. Similarly, Mildred Bailey is widely recognized as the very first Big Band female voice. And, as Mildred's husband, Red Norvo, testified to me recently, earlier innovators Bessie Smith and Ethel Waters unmistakably influenced her career. Fittingly, Bing acknowledges his obligation to dynamic pre-Big Band song-belter Al Jolson. Facts now certified, we present this mini-treatise on the two of the most popular singers ever Al Jolson and Bing Crosby.

– AL –

My personal introduction to Al Jolson's repertoire of songs occurred in 1946 when Columbia Pictures produced an autobiographical movie entitled *The Jolson Story*. In this terrific film, Larry Parks, a tall and handsome actor with shocks of wavy hair, lip-synced Jolson's timeless songs while Jolson actually sang them off camera. Parks' bearing and acting ability was so convincing that, when I later saw actual photos of Jolson, I couldn't believe that Jolson was short, bald, diminutive, and, by this time, well beyond middle-age: sixty to be exact.

Parks' portrayal paved the way for a renewal of Jolson's tumultuous, egotistical career. Jolson became a reborn performer in the image of Larry Parks. His records sold in the millions once again. A new generation had discovered the old Jolson classics previously communicated to his audiences from elevated proscenium stages of vaudeville theaters

1

**An original music man, Al Jolson, photographed by Florence Vardamm.
(Richard Grudens Collection)**

and music halls where he had to shout over the heads of musicians in the orchestra pit to an expecting crowd: *My Mammy, Waiting for the Robert E. Lee, Avalon, Liza, California Here I Come, My Blushin' Rosie, Swanee, April Showers, Toot-Toot-Tootsie, and Rock-a-Bye Your Baby with a Dixie Melody.* Jolson's countenance was eternally eager; his need for an audience's love, desperate. He broke the barrier, constructing intimacy between an audience and a performer for the first time as he strode the runways.

The film elevated my interest in singing and singers. At a boy-scout jamboree amateur show I did the Larry Parks thing with a portable phonograph playing the movie's sound-track songs behind the curtain. I donned a black face and reflected on one knee emulating Jolson's *My Mammy.* I was fourteen.

Columbia followed with a successful sequel, *Jolson Sings Again.* Bing was heard in that movie singing *Learn to Croon* in one scene, but not seen.

Bing Crosby's singing methods juxtaposed Jolson's except that Crosby embraced the "new-fangled" electric microphone, directly and confidentially delivering his rich baritone voice into this new contraption, whereas Jolson's larynx was the only microphone he knew. Both were productive singers, Jolson beginning as an interpreter of Southern songs *a'la* Stephen Foster and Crosby at first imparting Fred Waring's Pennsylvanians type music with songs like Irving Berlin's *All Alone.*

The world came to know Al Jolson as *the* Jazz Singer. He was a rich and complex character who concentrated on delivering energetic performances, slowly climbing from obscurity as the son of Moses Reuben Yoelson, a dedicated sixth Cantor in an unbroken line of descent, to international fame and fortune. Jolson belted out his songs, usually first calling out his famous catch-phrase "You ain't heard nuthin' yet!" while thrusting his arm forward and across his chest and back out again, then shifting his body from side to side. Although Jolson mostly shouted his music from stages into live audiences, his recording career, first with RCA, followed by Columbia and Brunswick, enjoyed equally great commercial success. His first recordings were snappy ragtime pieces. Bing first recorded with Columbia singing selections *I'm Comin' Virginia* (arranged by my genius friend Bill Challis), *Side by Side, My Blue Heaven,* and other pseudo-jazz softies with Paul Whiteman's Orchestra.

3

Born in Washington, D.C., Asa Yoelson became enamored by performers who worked in local burlesque shows. He would visit his neighborhood Bijou theater and watch the popular drama *Uncle Tom's Cabin* and *Ten Nights in a Barroom*. As a child, Asa sang on street corners for coins, once attracting the attention of a Fagin-like character who encouraged him to try out his soprano voice in a show called *Rich & Hopp's Big Company of Fun Makers*.

After that, nothing could keep him away from Washington area theaters. He admired the baggy-trousered comedians and vaudeville singers. On several occasions he sang with some of the performers when they requested the audience to join in. This, along with his father's scolding, his sister's nagging, and the ever-present Hebrew lessons, tested his patience so he ran away from home to become a vaudeville performer. He was twelve.

Al Jolson was brought back home time and time again but continually ran off to join various show business endeavors. His father whipped him, but he always returned to the Bijou, hoping to follow his dream. At fourteen, Baltimore became his delinquent destination, working there as a singing waiter. His father found him, forcefully accompanying him home. Asa wanted to sing in a theater, but his father desired him to sing in the synagogue as the seventh cantor in that unbroken family line.

For months afterwards he constantly ran away but was recovered. Desperate, his father enrolled him in a strict Catholic school. Even that could not hold him. Then he was off to New York, sleeping on a bench in Central Park and having his shoes stolen while sleeping. Going back home was now impossible, so he found the nearest eating place where he traded for food and shoes by dish washing and sweeping, with a song or two thrown in.

He sang anything, anywhere. He knew his voice was good. In the theatrical district he worked for six dollars a week. Unfortunately, booking agencies rejected him because of age and lack of experience. A meager existence was eked out during the next few years—his destiny to sing held tight in his heart. He always pictured his name in lights. Singing was sometimes accomplished in Coney Island side shows, encouraged by requests from individuals who enjoyed listening to the little boy with the tremulous voice.

– BING –

Harry Lillis "Bing" Crosby came to light in Tacoma, Washington, on May 3, 1903. Some, including Bing himself, always thought he was born on May 2, 1904 (because of lost records), but Ken Twiss (late President of the former Bing Crosby Historical Society), myself, and many other Crosby aficionados have since unmistakably proven to the world Bing's correct and verified birth date of May 3, 1903.

Bing was first a drummer. Yes, a drummer! I witnessed Bing's drumming in the 1940 film *Rhythm on the River.* He tapped drum and cymbal rhythmically to the title song while vocalizing and marching around a pawn shop with a few other musicians including Wingy Manone and Harry Barris:

> *When you hear a real hep-cat*
> *Take a chorus in A flat,*
> *That's the rhythm on the river,*
> *You know what that means, he comes from New Orleans!*

The sobriquet "Bing" was acquired from a comic strip called the *Bingville Bugle* which he enjoyed so much and was likened to as a child of seven. In school he enjoyed the art of diction and phrasing, techniques he mastered in elocution contests. A busy and hard working kid, Bing Crosby's happiest job was as a prop assistant in the Auditorium, Spokane's big opera house. It's here his favorite singer, Al Jolson, performed while touring in the Broadway shows *Sinbad* and *Bombo.*

"Later, when I got to know and work with Al, he didn't remember me, the lop-eared lad named Crosby who watched his every move, but I remembered him vividly," Bing recalled in his 1953 autobiography, *Call Me Lucky,* "You could never forget Al Jolson. He was absolutely electric! When he stepped onto the stage and started to sing, young and old were immediately captured by him. He was irresistible."

Crosby organized a quartet who joined a band called the Juicy Seven, playing drums and singing. While a student at Gonzaga University he ran away, hitchhiking to California, but was driven back by hunger, not unlike his hero, Al Jolson. Returning to school, he nervously sang his first solo, *For Me and My Gal,* with the band. Al Rinker, singer Mildred (Rinker) Bailey's brother, invited Bing to join in his

5

band. He was excited by Bing's drum playing and vocal ability. The group was called the Musicaladers. They began playing at high school dances. When singing *For Me and My Gal* with the aid of a megaphone, he started his signature "ba-boo-ing" when he forgot some words. Bing once told his mother that he'd rather sing than eat.

After a few local restaurant gigs, Mildred invited her brother and Bing to come to Los Angeles to try their luck performing in speakeasies. It was Crosby and Rinker, two boys with a piano playing first at the Lafayette Cafe in Sacramento with Al at the piano and Bing scat-singing while tapping a cymbal. In April 1926, the boys were hired to sing at the Metropolitan Theater in a variety show at $65 weekly each. *Variety* dubbed them a success in an unsuccessful show. The amiable, easy-going Bing was a hit.

– AL –

In Jolson's world, twenty -five years earlier, it was the turn-of-the century and the golden age of vaudeville. Theaters abounded in every city. Jolson's persistence finally paid off when he paired with his brother, Harry, in an act under the auspices of the fledgling William Morris Agency. The association with this agency lasted his entire career. They played all the houses in Brooklyn and Manhattan and carried the act to Philadelphia and Pittsburgh. In-between acts Al Jolson would deliver his songs. Although sometimes appreciated, he was more often hooked off-stage with tomatoes and eggs tossed at his heels.

Jolson's professional career began earnestly one night in San Francisco at the Globe Theater. Arriving there right after the 1906 earthquake, he stayed on developing his craft and establishing himself for the first time as a straight singer. Then it happened, unexpectedly and suddenly. Al's backstage "dresser" was a black man named Ezra who suggested Al spruce up his otherwise mediocre act by blacking his face with burnt cork and singing songs in the true Southern style. He followed Ezra's instructions and went on one night with trepidation singing, "Rosie, you are my posey—you are—my heart's bouquet..."

It worked. The audience went wild. He strutted up and down the stage in white gloves and rolling eyes, shuffling and waving gestures. The singing was inspiring. The songs went straight to the heart of the vulnerable audience who recalled him from backstage for encores. His

Al Jolson and his wife Ruby Keeler 1932. (Movie Star News)

dream was at last realized. Blackface would be his new mark, and word spread in theatrical circles. One night, famous producer Lew Dockstader of Dockstader's Minstrels approached him backstage resulting in Al Jolson's first important singing contract.

Apprenticeship in Dockstader's was short-lived as the impatient Jolson wanted to change the act, expanding his vocals into the new "jazz" idiom. He headed back to New York, encouraged by Lee Shubert of the famous show business empire. Once he sang *Alexander's Ragtime Band* for Shubert's skeptical partner, Arthur Klein, Jolson's power burst forth. Klein excitedly stood up saying: "Now *that's* singing!" The timbre and technique entranced the partners and Al Jolson was on his way to becoming the biggest name in show business.

On March 20, 1911, Al Jolson made his first Broadway appearance (in blackface—against his producer's wishes) in the show *La Belle Paree,* singing clearly and vibrantly *I Want a Girl Just Like the Girl that Married Dear Old Dad* at the Winter Garden Theater in New York before critics and the cream of New York theatergoers. Like the later Crosby, Jolson was at first very nervous, but his performance was a revelation. Singing never sounded like this on Broadway. He began singing more songs than were scheduled: "Oh, Susanna, Oh, don't you cry for me," and "We will sing one song for my Old Kentucky Home"—and more. He shuffled across the stage, his voice rich and sweeping. Finishing off the performance with a long, rousing version of *Dixie,* Al Jolson knew he had made it at last. He was ecstatic. So was the audience. A new twenty-six year old singing star had arrived on the scene and would remain for the next twenty-five years.

It was the competitive era of sexy Mae West; Pat Rooney's soft shoe, Sophie Tucker's *Some of these Days,* Ed Wynn's comedic madness; the great Sarah Bernhardt performing at the Palace with W.C. Fields; Scottish star Harry Lauder singing *Roamin' Through the Gloamin',* and the genius of Charlie Chaplin. Jolson was king of them all. Crosby was a wannabe kid watching from the wings. Bing and the world had latched on to a meteor speeding through space.

In show after show Jolson would always come back on stage after the last act, and, following no set script or schedule, would sing one song after another, accepting requests from individuals in the audience: *You Made Me Love You* and *Oh, You Beautiful Doll* were numbers sung out with typical Jolson gusto and boundless energy, "Folks, now don't go away. It's only 11:30 and you ain't heard nuthin' yet". There was no stopping him as he often sang to beyond the midnight hour. He was earning over $2,000.00 a week, an unheard of salary of the time.

During World War I, Al Jolson received an invitation to the White House to lunch with an admirer, President Woodrow Wilson. Al's father was amazed and proud: "Only in America are such things possible," he said proudly, "Maybe I had been wrong about Asa becoming a cantor after all."

The show *Sinbad,* again at the Winter Garden Theater—a place now synonymous with Jolson—was to be the crowning achievement. He opened with *Rock-a-Bye Your Baby with a Dixie Melody* and followed with *Hello, Central,* and *Give Me No Man's Land,* in the best Jolsonesque manner. The show was the talk of New York. Performances were sold out. Jolson burst forth in full force with patriotic numbers, Richard Whiting's *Till We Meet Again,* Billy Baskette's *Good-bye Broadway, Hello, France,* and Irving Berlin's *Oh! How I Hate to Get Up in the Morning.* All were smash hits, as was George M. Cohan's great wartime song *Over There.* Then, young songwriter George Gershwin asked Jolson to sing his new song *Swanee,* composed for his first Broadway show *La La, Lucille.* Jolson was exactly the right performer to put over this song.

"Folks," Jolson said as he greeted the audience after the regular show ended, "I have a new song for you tonight. It was written by a dear pal of mine—a young fellow you're going to hear from quite a bit, George Gershwin. The song is called *Swanee.*" The audience applauded in honor of the composer; then Al, still in blackface, went into his song. *Swanee* became an instant Jolson classic and helped catapult the career of George Gershwin.

In 1920, the song *My Mammy* was selected by Jolson for his opening number one night during the run of *Sinbad.* There were doubts about featuring the song among the owners and producers, but the catch in Jolson's voice...the sobbing sound that cried out to the audience, created an impact. Ladies cried and men's lips trembled as he delivered his song. Down on one knee, Jolson stretched out to them:

9

"I'd walk a million miles for one of your smiles.....my Ma-ma-a-my." They melted. They screamed, demanding encores. It was a nothing less than a triumph.

– BING –

In 1926 Bing Crosby and Al Rinker began unleashing jazz rhythms into their act with enthusiasm and tricky harmonies. Then, the break: Paul Whiteman and his King of Jazz orchestra arrived in LA. His emissaries were sent to evaluate their act. The audition earned them a contract at $150 a week for five years. In Chicago: "I want to introduce two young fellas who have joined our band," Whiteman declared from center stage, "I picked them up in an ice cream parlor in a little town called Walla Walla, and I brought them to you. They were too good for Walla Walla. Meet—Crosby and Rinker." They were simply excellent, and like the early fledgling Jolson, encores were demanded from the crowd. In New York, at the Paramount in 1927, they added Harry Barris to the act at the suggestion of Matty Malneck, a song-writer and Whiteman reed musician. Later, the trio performed twice a day for a year without Whiteman (who went touring in England), on the Keith-Albee-Orpheum vaudeville circuit. They partied excessively and got into some minor trouble with the law along the way. When Whiteman returned, they all went to Hollywood and made the film *The King of Jazz*. Bing, Harry, and Al, the Rhythm Boys, sang the landmark number *So the Bluebirds and the Blackbirds Got Together* (with a Bing solo), *A Bench in the Park* and *Happy Feet* with the Brox Sisters. Crosby earnings climbed to $400.00 a week working for Whiteman at the Cocoanut Grove nightclub. It was there Bing met his future wife Dixie Lee.

Guitarist Eddie Lang and jazz violinist Joe Venuti joined with Whiteman and became close lifetime friends with Bing. After leaving the Whiteman organization, the Rhythm Boys reformed and successfully plied their act at the Montmarte Cafe. In-between gigs Bing acquired small parts in movie shorts. His good looks and geniality won over many new fans. Shortly thereafter, Bing recorded *I Surrender, Dear,* his first hit in a Sennett film followed closely by *Just One More Chance,* a Brunswick label solo. And, notably for the newly independent trio, they recorded Harry Warren's *Three Little Words* with Duke Ellington and his famous Cotton Club Orchestra.

On November 23, 1931, Bing recorded his lovely gem, *Where the Blue of the Night Meets the Gold of the Day,* his lifetime signature vocal.

– AL –

Al Jolson went on to sing the best songs of his lifetime on stage, in the movies, and on the radio. He was selected to sing in *The Jazz Singer,* the first notable talking movie. It was a risky experiment, but Al was always willing to gamble even though others had turned down the role. It was 1927. Lindbergh had crossed the Atlantic while *The Jazz Singer* premiered at the Warner Theater in New York, where young, brash Bing Crosby was just beginning his recording career. Jolson was hailed as the "Lindbergh" of talking movies, the man who had ushered in a new type of film entertainment. The three million dollars earned was a record for a low-budget film. In a subsequent film *The Singing Fool* Jolson emoted on the tear-jerker *Sonny Boy.* Sheet music and records of the song sold like hotcakes. Every studio was now making "talking" pictures. Al Jolson was now the infallible giant of show business.

Al Jolson's reign would last until an amazing wave of new talent began to eclipse his formula. First, radio stars Rudy Vallee ("Hi, ho, everybody"), Edgar Bergen and Charlie McCarthy ("Step aside, Bergen"), George Burns and Gracie Allen ("Say good-night, Gracie"), Jack Benny ("Oh, Rochester, will ya start the Maxwell?"), Kate Smith (*When the Moon Comes Over the Mountain*), Eddie Cantor (*If You Knew Suzie like I Know Suzie*), Cecil B. DeMille ("Lux presents Hollywood"), and former Jolson emulator Bing Crosby invaded Jolson's professional space. A fickle public now focused on these new prime-time radio entertainers performing in their own living rooms, communicating from aesthetic consoles or simple, inexpensive tabletop radios.

Concurrently, movie theaters featured Tony Martin, Don Ameche, Gary Cooper, Nelson Eddy, Fred Astaire, and the great John Barrymore. Jolson was no match for these articulate, romantic leading men. Third, musically, Paul Whiteman, Glen Gray and his Casa Loma Orchestra, Louis Armstrong, Mildred Bailey, Duke Ellington, The Boswell Sisters, Billie Holiday, Benny Goodman, and, again, Bing Crosby completed the eclipse.

Even Jolson's marriage to singer-dancer Ruby Keeler, whom he once rescued when she was faltering during a song while performing in a Broadway show by standing up in the audience and singing her part from his seat while she recovered and continued, now overshadowed his career. While she was cast in top movies like *42nd Street* and *Gold-Diggers* of 1933 with Dick Powell, Jolson was doing bit parts on Bing's Kraft Music Hall radio show and backup roles singing in minor films. She was America's sweetheart while he became Mrs. Ruby Keeler.

"I've heard a lot of talk from people about what a break it was for Al Jolson when I gave him time on my radio show. Actually, signing him was a lucky stroke for me. Some of the best shows I've ever had involved Al. If they helped Al make a comeback—they helped me as much," Bing Crosby explained, "Al happened to me at a time when I needed good shows, and getting him to go on with me gave me a big boost."

Al Jolson did a valiant job entertaining troops during World War II under the auspices of the USO. He was the first notable entertainer to tour the front lines. The song *Sonny Boy* became the G.I.'s favorite. After the war, Columbia gave him a perfunctory position as a film producer. The general inactivity bothered him. He didn't like TV, feeling good performers dissipated material and routines developed over years on one single TV shot and then drove themselves crazy trying to develop something fresh every week.

In the spring of 1946, Jolson received an interesting call from assistant Columbia producer Sidney Skolsky. "Al, may I have a word with you?"

"Sure."

"Al, I have an idea that might be a big thing. A remake of *The Jazz Singer*.....you know, it's the 20th anniversary of talking pictures."

"I'm listenin'. Achin' all over for good ideas."

"Well, it would be the story of your life."

"It's old hat. Who the hell wants to go through my life again?"

"I know, but do I have your blessing?"

"Sure, but everybody knows I'm a has-been."

"You won't actually be in it, but, well—I'll tell you later after I get an okay."

That conversation led to the development of the film *The Jolson Story,* acted through by Larry Parks, coached and actually sung by Jolson himself. As always, Al Jolson gave it all he had and it worked. The picture had tremendous impact on movie audiences. Besides a renewal of his outstanding career, Jolson earned a cool million dollars.

– BING –

Meanwhile, Bing Crosby was busy climbing music's golden ladder. By the time *The Jolson Story* was playing on movie screens in 1946, Bing had evolved as America's most important crooner, to be later followed by *his* emulators Frank Sinatra, Perry Como, Frankie Laine, Tony Bennett, Pat Boone, Dean Martin, and Elvis Presley, who all did pretty well. I wrote briefly about this in my first book, *The Best Damn Trumpet Player.*

Along the way Bing amassed a long list of sturdy standards: *I Surrender Dear, Please, I Found a Million Dollar Baby, Melancholy Baby, Pennies from Heaven, Just One More Chance, I'm Through with Love, Sweet and Lovely, Where the Blue of the Night Meets the Gold of the Day, June in January, I've Got the World on a String, Sweet Leilani,* and in 1942, Irving Berlin's now world-famous song, *White Christmas,* a landmark Crosby recording. Of course, there were hundreds of hits. What's your favorite? I've listened to those Crosby recordings for an entire lifetime. They satisfy. That's why my personal encounter with Bing Crosby at NBC's New York studios in 1952 left me so breathless. I was just a kid in an NBC Page uniform, but I realized the existence of his legacy even then.

After careful consideration, I determined my favorite Crosby film song to be Cole Porter's anti rock-and-roll song *Now You Has Jazz,* performed with Louis Armstrong and his All-Stars in the acclaimed film *High Society.* A mature, jazz oriented Bing loosely flings his arms and breezes through this hip tune supported by Satchmo and his great musicians which included my longtime friend Arvell Shaw, Louis' longtime bass player. Louis and Bing genuinely liked one another, another reason the song was executed so well.

My favorite Crosby singles in no particular order are *Shine,* with the Mills Brothers; the 1932 version of *Please; South America—Take It Away* with my pal Patty Andrews and her sisters; and *Swinging on a*

Bing Crosby, Decca President Jack Kapp and Harold Arlen scan
The Eagle and Me **song sheet. (Sam Arlen Collection)**

Star from the film *The Bells of St. Mary's,* a song I always tried to sing to my kids when I could get them to listen. Like a true Crosby aficionado, I've enjoyed almost everything he has ever recorded. As a lifetime Jolson fan, the story is the same. Of the roughly 569,400 hours I've been on this earth, I calculate 23,725 combined hours have been logged listening to Bing Crosby and Al Jolson. A perfect pastime, worth every moment.

Bing performed in many films beyond all those early Mack Sennett shorts. First, a starring role in *The Big Broadcast;* then *Going Hollywood;* Mississippi; *Rhythm on the Range; Pennies from Heaven, Waikiki Wedding; Rhythm on the River;* all those seven wonderful *Road* pictures with my friend Bob Hope and sarong-sporting Dorothy Lamour. We cannot forget the later *Holiday Inn; Going My Way* (his Academy Award Best Actor winning role); *The Bells of St. Mary's; Blue Skies; Welcome Stranger* (I loved that charming film in which Bing sings *My Heart Is a Hobo* to Barry Fitzgerald); *Riding High; Little Boy Lost;* and *White Christmas* with Song Star Rosemary Clooney and Danny Kaye. And, of course, *High Society* with Grace Kelly, Frank Sinatra, and you know who. Bing told my friend Jack Ellsworth in 1976 that his own personal favorites were *My Isle of Golden Dreams* and *There's a Cabin in the Pines.*

Bing Crosby loved singing since he was a little boy, and he did it with ultimate ease, but he enjoyed sports just as well. The consummate sportsman, he recorded mostly in the morning and usually in one take, according to Patty Andrews, because, as she explained to me: One, "Bing believed his voice possessed a husky quality early in the morning—on an empty stomach. I guess he used to vocalize in the car on the way to the studio," she revealed, "and he always wore his golf clothes." Bing was an avid fisherman, hunter, golfer, and baseball fan. (Bing owned 20% of the Pittsburgh Pirates in 1947 and 10% of the Los Angeles Rams Football team in 1949)

Would there have been a Crosby without an earlier Jolson? Jolson was the very first pop singer, wasn't he? Did he pave the road for Crosby's successful journeys? Scholars of the genre' say *yes!* Bing, himself, says *yes!* I absolutely agree!

– EPILOGUE –

Would there have been a Sinatra without a Crosby? Hard to say. According to Sinatra: "Crosby was my hero, the father of my career," Frankie Laine told me he consciously imitated Bing perfectly during Frank's marathon dancing days, and Tony Bennett admitted to me he was influenced "by Bing's casual way with a ballad. He enhanced my interest in singing." Pat Boone and Dean Martin have acknowledged they copied Bing's style too, as did Elvis with *Love Me Tender* and *Can't Help Falling in Love with You.* Then, to conclude, Jolson and Crosby combined were indeed the foundation of popular singing.

Al Jolson's songs are, of course, timeless classics. *Swanee* and *April Showers* are deeply carved in melodic stone with the *Anniversary Song* and *Avalon* (a jazz standard about a resort spot on California's Catalina Island popularized by Benny Goodman's Quartet) close seconds, *Sonny Boy* and *My Mammy* stand in an emotionally charged third place. *I'm Always Chasing Rainbows* and *Alexander's Ragtime Band* wrap up my list of favorites. Bing and Al definitively recorded *Alexander's Ragtime Band* as a duet in 1947 from a *Philco Radio Time* program.

The song production combination of Al Jolson and Bing Crosby cannot be overstated here or elsewhere. Personalities and private aspects aside, these two giants of the musical world set the stage for almost every subsequent male singer. Jolson and Crosby struggled during each of their career's formative years, but eventually rose to the pinnacle, their own personal Mt. Everest. Both voices will surely be heard far into the 21st century when the world may be listening to God knows what kind of music. Perhaps recordings featuring Bing Crosby and Al Jolson may be re-issued on electronic laser coins controlled by magnetic body implants or some other futuristic electronic conveyance so the music may be imbued directly into the brain—for the presumed then starving faithful.

Bing: "Al, you are indefatigable. If I'd let you, you'd sing all night."

Al: "You're no slouch, Bing. Never seen you nappin' over a song, you dog!"

16

A LETTER FROM KATHRYN CROSBY

Something Special about Bing

The preceding chapter about Al Jolson and Kathryn's beloved Bing was presented to Kathryn upon its completion. As a consideration of respect, and as a policy to insure accuracy, I always try to present the subject, or someone close to the subject, with my written material before publication to hopefully verify available information on a given subject. Kathryn graciously reviewed the material and after a wait of just a few days, sent the ensuing letter direct from her heart:

Dear Richard,

I have nothing of moment to add. As usual you've hit the nail on the head, and I'm just an observer, without your research or expertise.

But now that I think of it, I might mention one small thing of which only a member of Bing's immediate family might be aware: He sang all day long—snatches of opera, foreign favorites, the latest rock numbers, even medleys of radio commercials.

At our home in Las Cruces, Baja California, Bing woke his friend Dr. Sullivan one morning with a fortissimo rendition of YOU CAN TRUST YOUR CAR TO THE MAN WHO WEARS THE STAR.

"If you want to appoint me your agent, " Sullivan mused, "I'll bet I can get you some bread for that sort of work,"

"Oh, I dunno, Bill," the assassin of sleep replied. "I hear they got their own fella."

And off he strode into the dawn, roaring out TOREADOR EN GARDE....

And how I miss him! And what I'd give to hear him saluting the sunrise with CIELITO LINDO just one more time!

Best Wishes,

Kathryn Crosby

Kathryn Grandstaff Crosby is a fine person and a singer in her own right. If you manage to find yourself a copy of *Bing and Other Things,* a book she authored in 1967, depicting her life before and after her marriage to Bing, you will get to know her a little and discover her unique qualities and understand why Bing became a lucky, happier, and wiser man the day he married her in 1957. An actress, registered nurse, wife, mother, she was also a teacher, a dress designer model, and an author. She remembers Bing's first words to her, "Howdy, Tex," he drawled, "What's your rush?" She was hurrying a load of petticoats to Paramount's wardrobe department.

Twenty short years later, after a wonderful life with Bing and their three children, Harry, Nathaniel, and Mary Frances, she, and we, lost Bing.

In her second book, *My Life With Bing,* Kathryn fervently noted: "His music lives, his films live, the gentle humor that he displayed is a touching living wondrous thing. His eyes will never dim and his beauty will never diminish."

**A young, smiling Dick Haymes at the height of his success.
(Richard Grudens Collection)**

DICK HAYMES

Helen Forrest and I, Keeping It Simple

When Helen Forrest and I wrapped up her chapter, "Voice of the Big Bands," prominently featured in my book about all the girl singers of the Age, *The Song Stars*, we promised one another to meet once again in honor of her favorite baritone and one time singing partner, Dick Haymes, recognized internationally as one of the most potent baritones of all time, to prepare a suitable chapter about him for this important book about the men singers. Helen's enthusiasm for *The Song Stars* book truly gratified me. "I loved the treatment of all the singers. Let's feature my friend Dick Haymes in your next book," she wrote, "I'll help you—and don't forget Don Cornell." We kept that promise on the afternoon of September 17, 1997.

Helen, recuperating from a nasty cold that had developed into a mild case of pneumonia, sipped on a tall glass of fresh orange juice while we exchanged pieces of substantive information about Dick Haymes' life and career.

Richard Benjamin Haymes came to first light on a family-owned cattle ranch in Buenos Aires, Argentina, on September 13, 1918, and emigrated to the United States when he was two. He traveled throughout Europe with his mother, a famous musical-comedy soloist and singing teacher, and mining-engineer father (who hailed from Scotland). Dick lived in Europe for five years, speaking both fluent French and Spanish. Attending Loyola College to be educated by Jesuit priests in Montreal, Canada, he again furthered his education in Switzerland. "This accounted for his cultured behavior, his gentlemanly bearing, and his obvious class," Helen said, "Dick Haymes was a man of class. No one would ever deny that fact."

Starting out as a songwriter with his brother Bob, Dick inadvertently wandered into singing after persuading the manager of a New Jersey summer resort to give him a job as the boy singer with the local band at the weekly pay of twenty-five dollars. Later, as a vocalist for Johnny Johnston, and later with Bunny Berigan, Dick eventually formed his own band he called The Katzenjammers for a short time.

Then Dick decided to hitchhike to New York to sell some of the songs he had written. He approached bandleader Harry James, who, it turned out, needed a singer more than a songwriter and, talk about good timing, hired Dick as the band's boy singer after hearing him demonstrate one of his songs at the Nola Studios where Harry was rehearsing. Frank Sinatra was about to leave the band, and Dick, walking in a long shadow, followed him into the bands of both Harry James and Tommy Dorsey. Sinatra always seemed to be a step in front of him, as he moved along in his own career.

Dick's recording of *I'll Get By* was a best-seller with James, where he was hailed as a fine singer who, week by week, improved his phrasing, shading, intonation and reputation. In May of 1942, after trying to form his own band, Dick joined Benny Goodman where he scored once more as a fine and sensitive vocalist with the songs *Serenade in Blue* and *Idaho*. In August of the same year Dick joined up with Tommy Dorsey just when the band left for California. MGM had signed Tommy and the gang for the film *DuBarry Was a Lady* and Dick also sang with the band during its nine week appearance at the Hollywood Paladium. But, the era of Big Band singers was winding down, and, for Dick, that either meant going solo as a vocalist or back to song writing and plugging.

"The experience with Harry was great because he had a new band and it was a new experience for him as well," reported Dick to author Fred Hall, "But, with Tommy—well Tommy's (Dorsey) band was the actual Tiffany of the orchestra world in those days—because he gave you a showcase. He was a star-maker because he said, 'Okay, here's your spot—do your song,' and he had arrangers like Sy Oliver, Paul Weston, and Axel Stordahl. I learned lessons in performing as well as singing and breath control. We had the cream of everything—this big, huge, wonderful orchestra. I lasted just two short years."

It was Helen O'Connell who told me that it was she who introduced Dick Haymes to her then manager Bill Burton. At the time, Dick was on the ropes career-wise, having sent his wife, actress Joanne Dru, and their son Skipper to New York to live in a furnished room, while Dick, remaining in a Hollywood hotel, tried to find suitable work, but was finding it difficult to sell his songs or skills as a soloist.

On Helen's word, Burton telephoned Dick and sent him funds to pay his hotel bill and carfare to come to New York. Burton also moved Joanne and Skipper into an apartment, all before there had even been a signed contract: "He's that kind of guy," Dick said admiringly.

Burton's management proved to be a good move. Dick was quickly re-employed. First, a spot at New York's La Martinique on 57th Street, then a Decca recording contract and a NBC radio show, *Here's To Romance,* followed by a screen test that led to movie appearances with 20th Century Fox studios where he rose to stardom very quickly.

As a result of Burton's efforts, Dick Haymes began enjoying great popularity due to the success of the films *State Fair, Diamond Horseshoe* and *The Shocking Miss Pilgrim.* "I loved doing Billy Rose's Diamond Horseshoe—great tunes," Dick told fellow writer and broadcaster Fred Hall during an interview in 1978, "It was just a fun movie, and one of my pets." The songs *The More I See You* and *I Wish I Knew* were beautifully sung in that film by Dick. The tunes *For You, For Me, Forever More* and *Aren't You Kinda Glad We Did* were from *The Shocking Miss Pilgrim,* which also starred Betty Grable. *State Fair* produced the hits *Grand Night for Singing* and *That's For Me.* "That was a one and only original score for motion pictures that Rodgers and Hammerstein wrote. I was pretty lucky with that one," Dick reported to Fred.

The weekly *Autolite Radio Show* days began Dick's long association with Helen Forrest: "They were days of joy for all of us who got along so well," said Helen, "Our guests, like Judy Garland, enjoyed the company of Dick and Gordon Jenkins." The 30 minute show was a Saturday night affair and achieved a number one spot in the ratings. "It was terrific fun. Dick was terrific and made work fun," Helen went on, "We'd each do a number, then a third number together, then some sort of specialty number Gordon would write, often with Matt Dennis and Tom Adair. Each week we had a different theme. With Four Hits and a Miss and Gordon's choir, we made wonderful music together. We got a marvelous sound from all the voices."

During the tenure of the Autolite show they shared from 1944 until 1948, Dick Haymes and Helen Forrest became very close, welding together a lifelong friendship: "When I became nervous before facing an audience—I would actually begin to shake inside—but Dick would always seek to distract me. He would talk about anything that came into his head. He would make me laugh so hard sometimes that I almost forgot my fear," Helen said, "But, I always recovered once I was out there and Gordie (musical director Gordon Jenkins) struck up my cue. I'd smile when glancing sideways towards the wings at Dick who grinned with satisfaction as my fears subsided. Fortunately, the audience never realized what was going on." Helen says her happiest moments were rooted in the Autolite radio days. "We came alive when we came on the radio every week," she recalled, "There will never be another musical era like those days in the history of popular music. That was it."

The show was heavily promoted. Dick and Helen toured extensively to expand the show's popularity. "The songs *It Had to Be You, I'm Always Chasing Rainbows, Long Ago and Far Away,* and our favorite duet of the time, *I'll Buy That Dream,* were some of the successful numbers we promoted at theaters in so many cities. *It Had To Be You* and *I'll Buy That Dream* each sold more than a million copies," Helen recalled. Almost every one of their shared photographs of that period illustrated the joy experienced by Helen and Dick. The gladness in their faces reflected the obvious proof. "I always wore bright colored dresses with ribbons in my hair. I felt so feminine around Dick Haymes. He always made me feel accepted. We genuinely liked and respected one another." Helen still projects that same kind of enthusiasm, even today.

Once, they were traveling on a plane and trouble developed. "I was terrified. Dick didn't blink an eye. He started to shake his coffee cup as though in terror. He started kidding around saying, 'Remember the records, Helen. They'll be here long after you're gone. You'll be remembered. But the headlines will go to me. I'm the movie star. They'll say Dick Haymes Killed in Plane Crash! Beneath the headlines, in very small type, it'll say Helen Forrest also Lost.' By this time I was cracking up with my hysterical laughter. Of course, we landed safely."

According to my friend, Song Star Margaret Whiting: "Dick Haymes had a great sense of humor. He sang with such feeling and with a terrific attitude. Dick had learned a certain way of breath control that produced a distinctive, masculine sound. He was a charmer, beautifully articulate and well educated. We worked together for one week in

Boston—nine shows a day—women just fainted. Dick was classy, and boy, could he sing." she said.

By that time Dick and Helen shared the same manager, Bill Burton. "I think in retrospect that more aggressive management would have propelled Dick even further—like in the movies—as Frank was pushed. Bill Burton was a good manager, but Sinatra's people were tougher, as was Frank himself. Dick was less aggressive, always feeling the stress of facing live audiences, but he had a richer voice and was handsomer. The ladies genuinely loved him. They would write him letters and call him up. When he left the studio, they would always be waiting for him—hoping for a chance to see him up close or get an autograph. It would be difficult for him to avoid them."

Recently, Frankie Laine and I had a long conversation about all the men singers he knew: "I think Frank Sinatra's life would have been different had Dick Haymes lived longer. I always sensed a promise of great things to come when I heard him sing. His voice was rich and warm, a great baritone with great intonation and projections of warmth."

The "voice" of the big bands, Helen Forrest.

Helen Forrest and I reminisced about our favorite Dick Haymes recording, *Little White Lies.* "*Little White Lies* was Dick's best. It was a last minute thing-an accident, Richard. Four Hits and a Miss was our backup singing group and Gordie and Dick put it all together right there in the studio—on the spot while we were there—because they had some recording time left over. Well, Richard, it sold well over two million, and it's funny, but Dick never really liked that song, although I did."

I sort of compare Dick and Gordon's recording of *Little White Lies* to Tommy Dorsey, Frank Sinatra and the Pied Pipers' recording of *I'll Never Smile Again,* I said to Helen. "I like that style of arranging. I remember when the record was released. I was just seventeen and in love with a neighborhood Scandinavian girl who unilaterally chucked me aside one day for a Scandinavian Adonis. I recall sitting on the cold front steps of my house staring across the street at her house, pouting and softly murmuring the poignant words to *Little White Lies* a hundred times well into the evening, feeling sorry for myself." Here, Helen laughs her famous laugh—but more gently than those earlier days. "Talk about being so willingly victimized by a song's emotional message," she said.

In January, 1942, *Metronome Magazine* conducted a reader's poll, a contest of sorts. Actually they called it a *battle* between all the male singers. Sinatra came in first with 512 votes. Bing scored with 408, Bob Eberly with 275, and Dick Haymes with 233. All others lagged far behind with double, then single-digit numbers. The previous year Dick was only seventeenth. So, Dick Haymes consistently moved up there among the top singers of the period. Of course, polls are merely popularity contests, not an objective evaluation of a particular singer's vocalizing qualities. My opinion is that there will always be a "selection" of singers to choose from at any given time. Tastes differ. I have met individuals who actually detest the singing styles of Crosby or Sinatra, preferring the much richer, soft and romantic ballads of a Dick Haymes or Bob Eberly. "I never met anyone who didn't like the voice of Dick Haymes," Helen declared.

In 1998, when this book will be published, The Dick Haymes Society will mark 25 years of celebrating the life and times of Dick Haymes. This organization is more than a fan club, it is dedicated to preserving the memory of not just Dick Haymes the singer, but Dick Haymes the man, and includes vignettes of the other wonderful singers and performers of the Big Band Era and beyond. In the United States, my friend Roger Dooner of Minneapolis is a co-organizer. In Great Britain, it is Maurice Dunn, Denis Brown, and researcher Clive N. Filler. Presently, our own gracious Helen Forrest is the Honorary President. "I like that," Helen said proudly.

The Society honors, besides Dick Haymes and individuals in his family, past and present: musicians, composers, arrangers, producers, writers, and anyone else they could find who ever worked with him, for him, or paralleled his career. The newsletters abound with words (weak and strong) about Dick, and others from all walks of life: Fans, Society members, disc jockeys, critics, columnists, artist and repertoire men (from record companies), interviewers, singers, musicians, managers, and general observers of the genre'.

Books and recordings (old and new) are reviewed; quizzes become interesting fillers; discographys are listed; old advertisements are displayed; appropriate cartoons proliferate; priceless photographs abound (Oh, those photos!); filmography documented; obituaries noted; tributes of entertainers of all kinds featured; old, interesting articles from newspapers and fan magazines are faithfully re-printed, and so much more. It's a wonderful showcase for the greatest music ever played or sung, taken from the point-of-view of one Dick Haymes and his times and the spirit of his overflowing, productive career. The Dick Haymes Society produces quality glimmers from the past for current review, leaving me and other readers, I'm sure, in the same condition: Refreshed and renewed about those admirable days of good music.

There has been a lot written about Dick Haymes' share of bad luck. Success didn't come easy, and keeping up didn't either. Problems stemmed from his involuntary avoidance of the draft (because he was not a U.S. citizen) which were converted to threats of deportation, as well as one too many marriages that became disruptive, expensive and draining. True, his sense of humor saved him sometimes, as well as his good will and generosity towards others, but historically Dick Haymes was a simple man in a very complicated and trying business, subject to the vagaries of show-business life and the fickleness of the public. Dick harbored bitterness when hurt, which affected his performances, especially later in his career while on the comeback trail, which, for him, was almost like starting over. His hide was not as thick as Frank Sinatra's, who was able to shrug off the poisonous innuendoes and even go on the offense, as he often did in his darker days. Dick swallowed those offenses, thereby weakening his defenses, exposing his tender hide. But, like most men, when adversity challenges, the spirit rises to the occasion. Dick always maintained the spirit. A basically shy man, the unfair pressures brought to bear against him were always forgiven through his later-developed spiritual renewal.

Always loyal, Dick Haymes kept friendships for life, no matter what cards life otherwise dealt him.

When Dick sang *Little White Lies, It Might As Well Be Spring,* or *The More I See You,* you can be sure no one else could mark those songs as their own, but Dick Haymes. Tony Bennett has *I Left My Heart in San Francisco;* Sinatra owns *My Way;* Bing's is *White Christmas;* Nat Cole has *Stardust,* all master interpreters indelibly marking their song. After all, isn't all that what this book's about?

Have you ever heard Dick's great Capitol albums of 1955 and 1956 with Ian Bernard's Orchestra? It is considered as two of the finest vocal albums ever recorded. His 1962 album *Richard—The Lion-Hearted* with Ralph Burns also excels.

The 1960's found Dick Haymes appearing in England, Australia, Africa, Europe, and Ireland, where he became a citizen in 1965. The beautiful 1968 album produced by Alan Dell called *Then & Now* helped Dick restart his career and led him to return to America.

Dick's last recorded album entitled *As Time Goes By* with Loonis McGlohon and his Trio became very popular and still sells today. "Many people think that Dick Haymes' career ended after *Little White Lies* in 1948 and don't know about all the great work he recorded later on. These albums show how well Dick was singing right up to his death, and it fills a large gap in most accounts of his career that seem to dismiss his productive later years." Roger Dooner wrote to me in November of 1997.

Despite comebacks on television in the 1970's, followed by successful nightclub engagements in New York, Los Angeles, and Las Vegas, Dick Haymes' health was failing as the '70s advanced. Dick Haymes passed away in March, 1980, from lung cancer. According to many dissonant voices, Dick Haymes could have become the premier singer of the century had he not submitted to some of his own personal weaknesses and had he been able to concentrate on solidly building and furthering his career. Who knows?

For Helen Forrest, myself, and a great many others, Dick Haymes was certainly a superior singer among singers. One of the great four: Crosby, Sinatra, Como, and Haymes.

Post script: *The Dick Haymes Society* can be found at 2951 Tyler St. N.E., Minneapolis, Minn. 55418, and in England at 16 Cradley Park Road, Dudley, West Midlands DY2-9SR. Send Roger or Maurice a letter.

The young Dick Haymes at rehearsal.
(Richard Grudens Collection)

Nat King Cole and Oscar Moore doing Harold Arlen's
It's Only A Paper Moon **1950. (Richard Grudens Collection)**

NAT KING COLE

Trio to Solo, the Whole Music Thing Was Natural With Maria Cole

In his autobiography, *Music Is My Mistress,* the great composer, bandleader Duke Ellington described Nathaniel Adams Cole's relationship with his then popular band singer, Marie Ellington:

".....she was so pretty that Nat Cole took one look at her, scooped her up, carried her off to the preacher, married her, and took her home to his beautiful Beverly Hills love-nest, where she listened to his love songs for the rest of his life."

Recounting this charming fable to Maria Cole recently while we talked at her Massachusetts home, Maria smiled: "Well, it's partly true. We met at the Zanzibar Club right after I had just been fired from the Ellington Band....because they found out (she chuckles) I was trying to get a job as a single (she grins), and we fell in love with one another. But, Nat was married and in those days you waited for an interlocutory degree in California. So it all took time."

Maria speaks so clearly and warmly, much like her beloved Nat Cole sang. Marie adopted *Maria* over *Marie* because she liked the way it blended with Cole. "It sounded more lyrical." Together they reared five children, three of their own and two adopted. First came Carol, who is Maria's niece, adopted when Maria's sister died. "Then Natalie was born, Richard," Maria said, "then nine years later we adopted our son Nat Kelly Cole, so-named in honor of St.Patrick's Day which was also Nat's birthday. Then came our identical twins three years later; Casey, named after our good friend (New York Yankees great) Casey Stengel, and Timolin, named after our very dear friend composer Johnny Burke's own little girl." Maria simply fell in love with the name Timolin.

We reminisced a lot about pianist /vocalist Nat King Cole this beautiful June day, about his phenomenal success rising first while backing jazz song star Billie Holiday on the piano as she performed her repertoire at Kelly's Stable nightclub in New York, to commercial success with his own jazz ensemble, The King Cole Trio, then ascension in a prolific career as a world-class soloist, producing an enviable list of standards to his credit.

"Nat had no particular favorite," Maria said, "although mine is *Our Love Is Here to Stay*. For Nat, the favorite was whatever was most popular at the moment. He loved every song he ever recorded."

We journeyed back to 1939, in Los Angeles, when Nat led his King Cole Trio, with Oscar Moore on guitar and Wesley Prince on bass. "Well, Nat's great piano influence was Earl Hines, "Maria recalled, "and so he loved playing piano and singing with the trio, but no particular singer influenced his singing career." With compact, syncopated backup chords and clean, spare, melodic phrases, Nat emphasized the piano as a solo, rather than a rhythm-style instrument in his arrangements. His playing complimented his singing—both completely being under his own control.

The vocals started accidentally while performing at various club dates. "Singing came very natural to Nat. There's a vast difference, if you listen, Richard, to Nat with the trio....with the kind of exaggerated Southern accent style compared to how polished he becomes through the years. It's fantastic." Nat had an uncanny ability to sit at the piano and sing with little effort. It was no problem for him at all. "He was a musician first, "Maria declared proudly, "and he *never* had a problem with breath control. Once Metropolitan Opera impresario Rudolph Bing, who was a fan of Nat's said—and I remember distinctly, Richard, exactly what he told Nat. 'Nat, come over and teach my artists some of your breathing techniques.' It was just a trick thing with Nat, I guess."

No less than Bing Crosby once added his "two cents" about Nat Cole. "I like to think of Nat Cole as a real strolling player—never pressing, never seeking for obvious effect, singing like he wanted no applause, cared little whether anyone was listening or not—singing because he liked to sing, because he liked the song. This fellow creates a wonderful mood anytime he works, I believe."

My initial interest in the King Cole Trio arrived with the recordings *It's Only a Paper Moon* and *Route 66*. Those songs suited his style perfectly.

Some accounts maintain that Nat Cole did not choose most of his material, and that he did not like to record the so-called rinky-dink songs *Nature Boy* (accompanied by his friend Frank DeVol), *Mona Lisa* (arranged by master arranger Nelson Riddle), *Ramblin' Rose, or Lazy, Hazy, Days of Summer,* but none of that is true, according to Maria. "He enjoyed all those songs very much. They were all hits. It wasn't a matter of liking a song—he picked them...he was smart...he could select good and commercially successful material. As a matter of fact, Nat did choose most of the songs he recorded."

**Maria Cole: Nat's wife, Natalie's mom and my friend.
(Maria Cole Collection)**

I handed Maria radio station WQEW's Listeners' Choice Countdown poll results for 1997, documenting Nat with the number two all-time winner among 156 recorded hits of the last 50 years: his stirring recording of *Stardust.*

"Richard, to me, no one has done *Stardust* like Nat." In the movie *My Favorite Year* Nat opens cold with Hoagy's (Carmichael) song *Stardust.* "Just get that movie—rent it—and listen to the way he sings that wonderful song. So crisp and clear. I can't explain it to you—you must listen for yourself." Nat also sang the rarely performed introduction to the verse. Hoagy Carmichael also said it was his favorite version.

Nat also captured 13th on that list with *Unforgettable,* 28th with *Mona Lisa, Unforgettable* again, at 48, but with daughter Natalie's voice over her father's original recording, which was released just last year for the first time. *Too Young* was number 49, *At Last,* number 98, *The Very Thought of You,* number 156—seven hits in all—not bad, I'd say. Maria looked approvingly at the list.

Composer, arranger Billy Strayhorn's masterpiece *Lush Life,* a very complex song, and so shunned by most singers, became another Nat King Cole achievement. "As everyone knows," Maria said, "it is a very difficult song to sing." But, Nat Cole clearly owns the definitive version of that song which Strayhorn had shelved for over ten years until he found Cole to record it for him to Pete Rugolo's fine arrangement.

Handful of Stars was another deep-rooted Cole classic. He managed that song as well as any crooner of his day. Nat's work with master arranger Nelson Riddle, who later did so much for Frank Sinatra's recording career, was exemplary as was his work with arrangers Gordon Jenkins and Ralph Carmichael.

Mel Tormé's *Christmas Song* is, of course, the song most identified with Nat:

"I was visiting my friend, Bob Wells' home in Taluca Lake for a work session," said the song's co-author Mel Tormé just a few months ago to my pal Mike Prelee, host of *In The Spotlight* on New Jersey's WVNJ, "I noticed a poem, written in pencil, resting on the piano music board;

Chestnuts roasting on an open fire
Jack Frost nipping at your nose
Yuletide carols being sung by a choir
And folks dressed up like Eskimos

"When Bob appeared, I asked him about the poem. 'I thought I'd write something to cool myself off this very hot day.' 'You know,' I said, 'this just might make a song.' We sat down at the piano, and wrote *The Christmas Song* in forty-five minutes—honest!"

**Smooth looking, smooth sounding, Nat King Cole early 1960's.
(Maria Cole Collection)**

Mel Tormé eventually took the song to Nat Cole, who fell in love with the tune. His recording was released in the late fall of 1946. We know the results of that session.

I was telling Maria that Kathryn Crosby revealed to me that Bing sang all day long when at home. He would vocalize radio commercials, the latest rock numbers and opera arias, as well as ditties, while in the shower or strolling in the garden.

"Nat never did that, isn't that funny?" Recalled Maria, "He would sometime stretch his vocal chords, you know that thing that singers do to clear their voice. We had a separate playhouse on our property where he would sometime rehearse."

Like many black performers in the fifties and early sixties, Nat Cole experienced the cruelty of bigotry, especially during the early days working Las Vegas nightspots. Black performers were paid less and kept out of the main hotels, except when they performed. They lived in separate quarters on the outskirts of town. "I didn't go to Vegas with Nat—when he first started there—because of the bigotry. He never subjected me to that. The only reason to discuss the bigotry that existed at the time is because he really did live through it. It's a shame he didn't live to see it change for black performers, as it is today."

Nat Cole's television show in 1957 was unfortunately short-lived. "...although Nat had lots of support," Maria said. "His many friends, like Frankie Laine, and a roster of great talent, appeared regularly on his show, but, he gave it up on his own because he said, ' Madison Avenue is afraid of the dark,' a well-known classic line used at the time." Frankie Laine and Maria Cole have been great friends ever since those days. When Nat Cole passed away in 1965, Maria gave Frankie a money clip that was owned by Nat, as a momento of his friendship with her husband.

Maria and I concluded that Nat Cole might have reached even greater heights as an entertainer were it not for the bigotry that existed during his lifetime.

In 1992, the Society of Singers in Los Angeles announced the first posthumous award in establishing the Nat King Cole Scholarship under the auspices of the National Foundation of Advancement in the Arts. As Society president Ginny Mancini said, "It was forty-five years ago between my daily rehearsals as one of Mel Tormé's Mel-Tones that Bob

36

Wells and Mel put the finishing touches on an inspired collaboration of melody and lyric that was to become a part of the tapestry of Americana. That was the birth of *The Christmas Song.*

"Each year, high school seniors having demonstrated exceptional vocal artistry will have an opportunity to participate in a national competition judged by professionals in the field, with the possibility of pursuing a meaningful (singing) career.

"It was my privilege to know him and experience first hand the incredible musicianship of Nat King Cole. It is an honor for me and the singers we represent to pay this tribute in keeping with his legacy."

The tributes to Nat King Cole have punctuated the years since his passing, his stature always growing. The latest was held at Carnegie Hall in a two day July 1977 celebration. Guest artists included the talents of Ruth Brown, Julius La Rosa, Mark Murphy, John Pizzarelli, Freddy Cole, Abbey Lincoln, Jon Hendricks, Jonathan Schwartz, and others who are happy to pay homage to one of the best singers ever.

When Nat Cole died, our mutual friend William B. Williams told Maria he would play a Nat King Cole record every day as long as he was on the air. And he did! It was a fact that Frank Sinatra proclaimed proudly during a tribute to William B. Williams.

Maria sums it up this way:

> *Nat was the kind of person who didn't have just one good friend—he had lots of friends—but he was not a person to hang out with this one or that one when he was off. All the guys loved him. Sure, he was on the road most of the time, but he was a wonderful husband and he loved all the phases of his life. For him the whole music thing was natural. He was a guy who went along with the program, a man who kept everything inward except his songs. He loved whatever he was doing, whenever he was doing it. He loved his career—he loved music.*

As a parting gift, Maria presented us with three wonderful photos, two of Nat King Cole that I have never seen before and one of herself. We have graced Nat King Cole's Music Men chapter with all three for you to enjoy.

On the set of Dean's TV show. L to R: Lee Hale, Orson Wells, Dean Martin, Producer Greg Garrison.
(Lee Hale Collection)

MY FRIEND—DEAN MARTIN

By Lee Hale

He was unique, one of a kind. Tall, dark, and handsome, Dean was a man's man and a lady's desire, and could sing as well as any singer of his day. Born Dino Crocetti in Steubenville, Ohio, Dean worked as both coal-miner and boxer, but decided to sing instead, and, according to every comedian he ever worked with, including his former partner Jerry Lewis, Dean was the world's best straight man.

Dean Martin first hit the big time when he teamed up with Jerry Lewis in East coast night clubs in the late 1940's. "I was supposed to be the singing half and Jerry the comic," Dean said, "and we both did a lot of both."

The boys began their ascent in show business. Their routines were almost always ad-libs. The on-stage antics had audiences howling. Fans began to expect the unexpected. Soon they completed a flock of hit movies for Paramount, and their appearances on NBC's *Colgate Comedy Hour* pushed them to the top of the coveted Neilson ratings.

Through all this, Dean was the anything goes kinda guy, while Jerry wanted to take charge, even produce, consequently reducing Dean's responsibilities. One day, and for no particular reason Dean could remember, the easy-going Italian crooner simply walked away.

"Everybody thought that was a big mistake on my part," Dean said, "after all, Jerry was supposed to be the funny one and I was just the straight man." Dean sashayed his way through a couple of forgettable MGM movies. It seemed the public assumed his career was over. But Dean knew better. Booked as a solo act in the best Las Vegas show-rooms, he found a *prop* that would establish his image from then on: a glass of scotch liquor. Vegas audiences, male and female, found him lovable. "I was just one of the guys," he would always say. That glass of scotch was mostly water. Some accused him of being a drunk, but Dean always said, "I would remind those people that I couldn't possibly do all the things I was doing if I were soused."

Some funny guest spots on a couple of TV specials led NBC to offer him a weekly hour of his own. It was the time, you know, when variety shows were the staple of prime time television. But Dean wasn't so sure he'd like fronting a weekly show. A lot of his co-performers had tried and failed (including Jerry), and besides, "Why would I want to waste six or seven days a week rehearsing. I had better things to do— like play golf—watch the soaps, or maybe do a movie or two." Dean pointed out. So he told NBC they could have him only if he didn't have to rehearse and if he could come in just one day a week, and that day had to be Sunday; and if they would also pay him a lot of money.

To his surprise, NBC said, "Yes!"

There was trouble at first. The bookings were fashioned around circus-type acts and Dean played Ed Sullivan: "And now, I'd like to present...." Maybe he'd sing a chorus of *That's Amore, Pennies from Heaven* or *Memories Are Made of This,* depending on how he felt that day. After the first show, with a multitude of pals including Frank Sinatra and Diahann Carroll, the ratings plummeted. The show's producer was fired and its director, Greg Garrison, assumed both jobs. With ideas on how to boost the ratings, he hired me as special material writer and musical director. We had to find a way to use Dean more and keep the one-day-a-week schedule.

I loved working with Dean Martin. We got along just fine. I figured out ways to work him into little routines with guests, and Greg stopped booking trained seals and trapeze acts. He brought in comedians, singers, movie stars and TV performers who seldom did variety shows. I would carefully rehearse the guests all week long, explaining they would have just one chance with him at the taping where he would be charming, gracious, and surprisingly easy to work with. Sometimes panic set in a guest the first time, but they usually returned in later appearances knowing exactly what to expect, happily going along with the unusual procedure.

It was discovered that the less Dean knew about the show, the more it became spontaneous and funny. Greg always kept the tape rolling, even the goofs, because Dean made his mistakes appear to be well-rehearsed. His experience with Jerry gave him an endless supply of one-liners and stock routines that could endearingly get him out of any awkward situation.

With Dean's easy-going manner and his fine singing voice, the ratings began to rise. Our experiment worked. Dean would arrive around noon Sunday for a snappy music run-through with Les Brown and his band. In his dressing room Dean would watch Greg and I go through his sketches and songs on a television monitor. Later, the audience filed into Burbank Studio #4 and the taping began. It took an hour to tape the show. Before the band finished playing the theme, our star was out of the studio and into his sports car.

Sure, Dean Martin was a major star, a wonderful singer, and a great nightclub entertainer, but, to me, it was the TV show that revealed the *real* Dean Martin. What you saw in your own living room was exactly the kind of guy he was; entirely likable, a terrific sense of humor, a perfect performer. Nobody will ever do what he did: pop in and do an hour's show without rehearsal and make it so entertaining.

For nine long years Dean Martin never balked at anything we threw at him—and sometimes those things were outrageous. Remember the time we had him slide down a pole and go straight through the floor, or when he jumped on his piano and it collapsed under him? Dean made my job easy. No matter what song we gave Dean, or what surprise guest appeared, he always performed with enthusiasm and excellence.

Oh, yes! I remember that Dean Martin did personally choose his one ballad in the middle of the show—you know, the one he'd sing with Ken Lane at the piano. You may also remember those ubiquitous cue cards on which he greatly depended, or the girls pushing him this way or that. Dean would stare at me offstage as I cued his entrances. Everytime he came out on the studio stage, he'd look around for me, "I owe my life to you out there," he once confided to me.

What fun we had. And what I'd give to bring back those glorious days. I sure miss my friend Dean Martin, one of the best singers ever.

Authors note: I have found a friend in Lee Hale. It was Lee who furnished us with his wonderful song *The Ladies Who Sang with the Bands* for our last book, *The Song Stars*. Besides his association with Dean Martin, Lee was once a singer himself, appearing with a group called the Manhattans, and was choral director for television shows *The Bell*

Telephone Hour and *The Entertainers*. After Dean's show, Lee produced NBC's historical *The First Fifty Years* which earned four Emmy nominations. Lee earned two, one for producing and one for video editing. Lee has been musical director for shows starring Bob Hope, Gene Kelly, Bob Newhart, and Jonathan Winters, gathering six total Emmy nominations. He has also created videos for Dick Clark, the Holland-America Lines, Princess Cruises and, of course, the Society of Singers where he sits on the Board of Directors. Lee is a great voice for our kind of music.

Epilogue: Comedian Dom De Luise, a frequent guest on the Dean Martin show, was appearing at Westbury Music Fair the night I interviewed music man Jerry Vale. Here's some of what he said to me about his friend Dean Martin, after I sequestered him into one of the prop rooms adjoining his dressing room:

"I was very nervous when I first appeared on Dean's show. He was an established star and I was very young and frightened. Producer Greg Garrison took me into Dean's dressing room. Dean was very sweet—he gave me a kiss and a hug—and was very kind to me. I was on and off his show for twelve years. Dean was very spontaneous—and he really didn't care what anybody expected him to do, so we would rehearse with Lee Hale doing Dean's part—Lee was in charge of all the music on the show and he would do it, but in a dry, adequate way. Dean would invariably watch it—then do it, having only come in the day of the actual show. Stars like Peter Sellers, Mickey Rooney, Jack Benny, Jimmy Stewart, and Kate Smith would work all week long. 'When is Dean coming?'—was always the question. In one sketch Dean was trying to mate his parakeet. The first line was—I would say 'How do you do?'—then Lee—behaving like Dean—would say, 'How do you do?' Then when Dean came in front of an audience, I said, 'How do you do?' and Dean answered, 'How do you do *what?*' The show was spontaneous even though we had rehearsed it. Dean would be doing it for the first time. I remember Dean being pushed this way and that—on his own show—by the girls or he looked offstage to Lee Hale—and

42

**Dom De Luise talks *Dean Martin* to Richard Grudens in prop room at
Westbury Music Fair in August, 1997. (Bill De Betta photo)**

even by one of the guests who knew where Dean should stand or
how or where he would move to. He loved it.

Dean was a family man, his children would come visit him all
the time, and, if you were sick, he would always call you. When
Dean lost his son, that was very sad because we all felt for him so.
There was a two week period where he didn't perform, and then he
went to Vegas. The audience knew he'd been through this tragedy,
and when he came out they cheered, applauded—I saw him weep
that night—and he started his routine and he was hysterically funny
and sang so well. At the end they gave him another ovation and he
cried again—and that was his re-entry from that tragedy back to
show business. He was sweet—without another agenda. He was
always right there for you—he always complimented me—on how
funny I was—and that was great. I once saw Dean sing a song and I
was very impressed. I went over to him and said, 'Dean, that was
great.' Now I had known him ten years—and I don't know how
many times I complimented him—and he said, 'Really! Was it that
good?' And I thought, 'Oh, my God! Here's Dean Martin—this big,

big star and he is cherishing my compliment'—which I really meant with all my heart, but I couldn't believe he needed it like I needed it. He was genuinely touched. And that's great to see that part of him. It was a gift from God to have worked with him and to have known him."

Thanks, Dom De Luise

**Legendary comedian Dom De Luise
and photographer Bill De Betta.
(Richard Grudens Collection)**

HAROLD ARLEN

Vocation: Writing Songs, Avocation: Singing Them With Sam Arlen

Over on Long Island's North Shore lies a beautiful house on a quiet street where the son of composer Harold Arlen lives among many momentos of his father's prolific career. I was introduced to Sam Arlen and his wife Joan by an old friend, Jerry Castleman, who is a fine contractor and has performed work for the Arlens including the building of a magnificent outdoor deck. The Arlens are regular suburban folks who are, however, staunchly dedicated to preserving the memory of Sam's famous dad, issuing CDs like the recent *Harold Arlen—Rediscovered,* released by his publication company S.A. Music in partnership with MPL Communications Inc. On them his father sings some of his own compositions. Thus, we have Harold Arlen, vocalist:

My pals Joan and Sam Arlen in the kitchen of their home on Long Island.
(Richard Grudens photo)

A very young aspiring singer, Harold Arlen.
(Sam Arlen Collection)

"Besides being a talented composer, my father was a very good song stylist," Sam and I were discussing his father's singing career on a very hot July summer afternoon during my visit to his charming home, "his vocal version of *Last Night When We Were Young* is my favorite of all his songs, Richard." Sam had set up a video program for me to observe and enjoy. There were interpolated clips of Harold Arlen singing his own compositions on *The Ed Sullivan Show* (*Let's Fall in Love* and *Between the Devil and the Deep Blue Sea*) and on a segment of Walter Cronkite's *20th Century* television interview program, filmed on location at Arlen's upper east-side Manhattan apartment. There were vignettes of home movies with his beautiful wife, Annie, as well and clips of visits by George and Ira Gershwin, among others, and even one with Sam as a child. This was the first time I had *heard* and *seen* Harold Arlen actually singing his own songs, including *Ac-Cent-Tchu-Ate the Positive, My Shining Hour* (my own personal favorite), and *For Every Man There's a Woman.* His phrasing was perfect for those compositions, and there were unmistakable implications of jazz in his delivery. You could tell he believed what he wrote and sang. One night recently I listened to it over and over. His was not a pop singer's voice, but more the unique sound of a Broadway musical protagonist, meaningful and serious when delivering his song's message, yet he started out as a band singer.

Harold Arlen was born Hyman Arluck, the son of a cantor, in Buffalo, New York, in 1905. At the age of seven he sang in the synagogue choir and began taking piano lessons. He responded to both the Hebraic religious chants and jazz. "My father gave me piano lessons so I could be a teacher and not have to work on *shabbas* (the Sabbath)," he once said.

Young Harold earned money playing in a silent movie theater and performing in a vaudeville act. At fifteen he formed the Snappy Trio with two of his friends. He became a singer and arranger with a band called the Buffalodians, filling engagements at college and society events. "I could always improvise," he said, "and I loved to invent unconventional tunes for the men to play." But, ironically, Harold Arlen's first ambition was to become a *singer.* He joined up with the Arnold Johnson band as an arranger and vocalist and wound up in the orchestra pit of the Broadway show *George White Scandals of 1928.*

But, he didn't do very well as a singer mostly because he felt that the demands of a singing career were, "something my temperament could not take," and so he concentrated on songwriting, which seemed to come to him more easily. His first important song was *Get Happy,* with Ted Koehler collaborating as lyricist.

George Gershwin praised *Get Happy,* a number which since has become a standard and is associated with Judy Garland (she sang it later in the 1950 film *Summer Stock*), causing Remick Publishing to offer Arlen a full-time songwriting job. Arlen later joined up with Ted Koehler at the legendary Cotton Club where they wrote songs for the Cotton Club Revues. They first composed *Between the Devil and the Deep Blue Sea* and *I Love a Parade.* Sam revealed a charming story about the song *I Love a Parade:* "My father loved to walk from his home to the Brill Building (in New York where all the song publishers are located) and Ted (Koehler) always took a taxi—even for a few blocks, rather than walk. My father encouraged Ted to walk for his health, and while on foot with him would start humming and imitating a marching drum, while Ted would chant, 'who needs a parade.' At the end of their walk, Ted asked Harold if he could remember the chant, a sort of a marching ditty—he did, and they worked it up into the song *I Love a Parade* when they reached the Brill Building."

The Cotton Club work also produced one of their best songs, *Stormy Weather,* which ultimately became a signature number for Lena Horne:

"Nobody could sing his songs the way he did," Lena said, "Have you any idea what a singer feels when she listens to him sing a song she has to learn? His range was phenomenal. You've got to be both intent and intense."

Back in vaudeville, Arlen became vocalist and pianist for Broadway song-belter Ethel Merman. He recorded the most successful rendition of *Stormy Weather* in 1933 with Leo Reisman's big band, his first ever recording of his own song. He also recorded with Red Nichols and his Five Pennies, Joe Venuti's Rhythm Boys, Henry Busse and his Orchestra, Eddy Duchin's Orchestra, and Benny Goodman. Those are big band vocalist credentials supreme, you have to agree. Still very few are aware of Harold Arlen's very expressive vocals.

When Hollywood signed up Harold Arlen, he produced nothing but grand slam home runs, writing songs for motion pictures. He earned an Oscar for *Over The Rainbow* from the classic film *The Wizard of Oz* and continued with songs *Blues in the Night* and *This Time the Dream's on Me* (with Johnny Mercer in 1941) for the film *Blues in the Night.* Endless compositions were written for films including *That Old Black Magic, One for My Baby,* and so many more.

While in Hollywood, Harold Arlen met and married Anya (Annie) Taranda. She was the first Breck Girl, (beautifully gracing magazine covers and television picture tubes), a Powers model, and an Earl Carroll's Vanities showgirl. They bought a house in Laurel Canyon, on Lookout Mountain, and lived there happily for 20 years.

But, this is a story about Harold Arlen, the singer, not the composer. Harold Arlen actually sang his own songs better than anyone else, in my opinion. Of course, by writing so many great songs, he supported so many other great voices. He was "the wind beneath their wings"—so the saying goes. There is no worthy singer who has not sung a Harold Arlen song at one time or another.

And Tony Martin told me this only a few days ago: "...he would interpret the songs for me when we were making the movie *Casbah.* In the song *What's Good About Goodbye* and *For Every Man There's a Woman,* he taught me how to vocalize those songs the way he intended them to be delivered." *Casbah* was the last movie score Arlen composed (with lyricist Leo Robin).

In fact, Sam Arlen says that many new singers are recording Arlen tunes more than ever before. The songs *It's Only a Paper Moon, I've Got the World on a String, I Got a Right to Sing the Blues, Let's Fall in Love, That Old Black Magic,* and *Come Rain or Come Shine* are regulars on recent CDs by a variety of artists, old and new.

Harold Arlen's biographer, Edward Jablonski, tells it this way: "He will close his eyes, cock his head, furrow his brow in deep concentration while his powerful yet sensitive fingers search among the seven white and five black keys.....and when he performs one of his songs, he becomes lost in the performance as he invests the lyrics with an impassioned delivery."

Sam Arlen says his dad had only one ambition not brought to fruition, "He would have liked to have written a serious symphonic work, much like Gershwin did with *Rhapsody in Blue* or arranger, composer Ferde Grofe' did with *The Grand Canyon Suite*. But he never got to it. "When his lovely wife died, Harold Arlen lost the major part of his creativity. He didn't accomplish much after that.

Sam surprised me when he turned up with some great photos of his dad with some famous friends. I had never seen them before. They are here for you to enjoy. He also handed me an original, hand-written original copy of *My Shining Hour*. Harold had isolated the closing phrase—"This will be our shining hour till we're with you again" and made copies for friends, tagging a Happy Birthday or other event, then signing and dating it. "I guess he realized how famous he and the song had become," Joan Arlen said.

Harold Arlen wrote over five hundred songs, thirty-six of them now considered classics. And we know he articulated every single one of his compositions at one time or another to either coach a singer, publicly perform, or simply enjoy them privately. His stature as a composer with

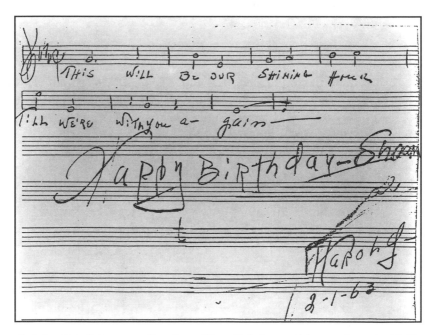

Original birthday greeting from Harold Arlen to his son, Sam, in 1963.
(Sam Arlen Collection)

his infectious melodies and sophisticated rhythms establishes him among the greatest of this century which includes Irving Berlin, Cole Porter, George Gershwin, Harry Warren, Vincent Youmans, Jerome Kern, Arthur Schwartz, Vernon Duke, Richard Whiting, Richard Rodgers, and Oscar Hammerstein. We lost Harold Arlen in 1986 at the age of eighty-one, but we will never lose his enduring music.

Sam and Joan Arlen are conscientiously keeping the Arlen torch alive.

A *Wizard of Oz* NBC broadcast. Standing L to R: (Lion) Bert Lahr, (Scarecrow) Ray Bolger, (MGM Exec.) L.K. Sidney, (Lyricist) E.Y. Harburg, Judy Garland and Harold Arlen at the piano. (Sam Arlen Collection)

**Der Bingle and Satchmo sing the *St. Louis Blues*, way back when.
(Richard Grudens Collection)**

SOME EARLY SINGERS

LOUIS ARMSTRONG—Player and Singer.

I guess you can say that Louis sang as well as he played. Did he play first, or sing first? No matter, he always sang. The legend of Louis dropping a songsheet and continuing on, thereby inventing what's called 'scat-singing' seems to be true, since I have read about it over and over. This was supposed to happen when he was performing with the Hot Five on a song called *Heebie Jeebies*.

Some purists were very unhappy when Louis sang more than he played later on in his career. He was considered by many as an artistic derelict. His singing emanated from his early cornet playing. Although his voice was untrained, he achieved vocals through shouting, but improved along the way arriving to his totally distinctive, instantly recognizable timbre. In some singer's recordings you have to stop and reflect, since so many singers of the era sounded somewhat the same, because emerging singers emulated one another, especially those that preceded them. But Louis' voice was unmistakable.

Songs like *St. James Infirmary* and *Basin Street Blues* are some early notable performances, yet nobody copied him. How could they without risking exposure as flagrant imitators. Louis grunted and gasped and distorted notes but always came back on track after straying way off. Billie Holiday did that too! *It's A Wonderful World* by Louis is the trademark recording that so easily identifies him to today's world.

The unmistakable sound of Louis Armstrong's gravelly voice is truly one of America's treasures.

TED LEWIS—Is Everybody Happy?

My introduction to bandleader and showman, singer Ted Lewis came from my mom, who adored him for a reason she never explained. He was a vaudeville star during Jolson's time. *When My Baby Smiles at Me* is his best-known composition and his theme. Ted had a dreamy delivery and always wore a battered top hat and sported a crooked cane as he vocalized while leading his band. He sort of talked-sang through his numbers, making you feel as though everything was going to be OK.

Ted began it all in 1916 with his first (only five members) band in Coney Island, Brooklyn, calling it Ted Lewis and his Nut Band. Benny Goodman once played with him, as did Jack Teagarden. He was one of the most popular 1920's bands. He played the clarinet, but not too well. His song *I'm Stepping Out With a Memory Tonight* drew tears on the Orpheum Vaudeville circuit when he talk-sung it. His film *Is Everybody Happy?* (a question he eternally asked his audience for over 60 years) for Warner Brothers in 1929 also did very well.

Ted Lewis retired at seventy-seven, making a final Las Vegas appearance at the Desert Inn. He passed from us in 1971 at his home in New York. He was 81.

RUDY VALLEE—Hi-Ho, Everybody!

Hi-ho, everybody! was his calling card. Hubert Prior Vallee captured the heart of an era with his Maine, New England twang: "I never had much of a voice. The one reason for my success was that I was the first articulate singer—people could actually understand the words."

Rudy Vallee enlisted the aid of a megaphone to project his voice forward in a time just before Bing Crosby embraced the use of the modern microphone. Bing Crosby acknowledged that Rudy broke trail for all the upcoming crooners. "He took up table singing up on the bandstand, and with blazer, megaphone, and a Yale education pioneered a lot of great hits," Bing once said.

Born in Island Pond, Vermont, in 1886, Vallee went to Yale University where he formed the Yale Collegians. He played the saxophone, drums, and various reed instruments. In 1928, he had his first break with his band at the Hi-Ho Club in New York City and was billed as Rudy Vallee and his Connecticut Yankees, leaping to enormous popularity including being carried over four large radio stations.

Starring in *The Vagabond Lover,* a film for which he wrote the title song, *I'm a Vagabond Lover,* elevated his popularity. Fleishman's Yeast sponsored his ensuing radio show that ran 10 years to his theme, *My Time Is Your Time.* Some say Vallee was responsible for promoting the careers of radio stars Eddie Cantor, Edgar Bergen & Charlie McCarthy,

Photo of original cover art of promotional *Hit of the Week* cardboard recording of Rudy Vallee 1929. One side photo, other side recording. (Richard Grudens Collection)

George Burns & Gracie Allen, and movie actress Alice Faye, when he featured them on his popular show.

In his later years, Rudy Vallee changed his image from a collegiate style singer to an austere rich man who seldom won the girl, and eventually became a successful comic actor in Frank Loesser's Broadway success *How To Succeed in Business Without Really Trying* in the early sixties. In Rudy's book, *Kisses & Tells,* he candidly blew the stardust off many of the celebrities he knew and worked with over the years. Rudy Vallee was the absolute Music Man of his Age. I always loved his rendition of *The Whiffenpoof Song,* never sung better.

OZZIE NELSON—Yes, Ozzie (and Harriet) Nelson!

In his early years, before Harriet Hilliard, Ozzie Nelson sang and recorded with his own band. That was 1937. Ozzie was sort of a Rudy Vallee type, also employing the use of a megaphone. They even resembled one another. His band contained some very good musicians. His major "sweet" band, that ruled the roost in those days before the advent of the Big Band Era, was second only to Guy Lombardo's and Eddy Duchin's. *Never in a Million Years, They All Laughed,* and *Head Over Heels in Love* were the songs that the head of the Nelson Family sang in 1937.

ARTHUR TRACY—The Street Singer.

Over the last few months I tried vainly to talk with Arthur Tracy, The Street Singer (from his film of the same name), as he was known back in the 1930's. One day he was sleeping, the next he wasn't feeling well. I never got to talk to him for more than a few minutes at a time. Unfortunately he passed away on October 5, 1997. Arthur was 98.

Born Abba Tracovutsky in the Ukraine, Arthur's family emigrated to Philadelphia. After some stints in vaudeville houses in and around Philly, William Paley of CBS heard him sing and gave him a job on radio. In 1931 he adopted the sobriquet "The Street Singer" uplifting his career. One of eight children, Arthur originally wanted to be an accountant, but, as he told me, he was offered a leading role in a Shubert Brothers Broadway production entitled B*lossom Time.* That led to film roles in *The Big Broadcast of 1932* with Bing Crosby. "I sang *Here*

Lies Love, but I did my role on Long Island and Bing did his role in Hollywood. We never met during the filming of that picture." he said.

Arthur is famous for wearing a wide brim hat and holding an accordion which he played while singing. His most famous song, *Marta, Rambling Rose of the Wildwood,* was recorded in 1931 and became a hit for him. Arthur sang in a homey, high tenor voice, and recorded prolifically: *Home on the Range, Love in Bloom, It's Easy to Remember, It's a Sin to Tell a Lie, Harbor Lights, The Last Time I Saw Paris, Red Sails in the Sunset,* and many more popular songs of the era. His richly romantic voice was coupled with Ruth Etting, The Boswell Sisters, The Mills Brothers, and even Al Jolson. London was his home from 1935 to 1939 for unnamed reasons. In England his recordings were well-known. He appeared in three British films: *Limelight, The Street Singer,* and *Command Performance.* Arthur had a resurgence of his career when his 1937 recording of *Pennies From Heaven* backed Steve Martin's early '80s movie. He then received offers to sing again. At the Cookery in New York's Greenwich Village, Arthur sang once again at the age of 82. Arthur received the Ellis Island Medal of Honor in 1995 along with Music Man Jerry Vale.

I had an odd affection for Arthur Tracy, perhaps because I remember my mother talking about him and dad always mimicking *Marta, Rambling Rose of the Wildwood,* the song most associated with him.

JACK TEAGARDEN—He was known inside the trade as Big T.

Jack Weldon Teagarden's uniquely developed style was widely imitated during his tenure with the big bands. Born in Texas in 1907, Jack Teagarden learned the trombone without any help whatsoever. Arriving in New York in 1927 at the age of twenty-two, Jack began his recording career, then advanced on to play in Paul Whiteman's famous King of Jazz Band beginning in 1933. After leaving Whiteman, Jack led his own band from 1939 to 1947, finally joining up with Louis Armstrong's All-Stars for four years, only to reform his band once again continuing on until his death.

Jack Teagarden was also an outstanding jazz singer. His engaging Southern drawl fell somewhere between Louis Armstrong and Bing Crosby, who were both his friends and his playing and singing partners, as well. Jack's demeanor and appearance, tall and handsome with a square jaw, open face and wide eyes he kept narrowed, occasionally made people take him for Jack Dempsey, the prize fighter. Some thought he was part American Indian, but his parents had come from Germany back in the late 1700's. His brother Charlie, a trumpeter, who also played with Whiteman, Jimmy and Tommy Dorsey, and Bob Crosby, was somewhat smaller. Jack became known as *Big T* and Charlie as *Little T.*

Jack's singing, a distillation of his sentimental playing form, was delivered in a light baritone combined with a Southern drawl, a kind of "lay-me-down-to sleep" style especially when he gathered friends around, first playing tunes like *I've Got a Right to Sing the Blues,* then vocalizing on it with accompaniment from sidemen. People liked Jack, he never displayed any conceit and never got on anybody's nerves.

According to Louis Armstrong's bass player Arvell Shaw, my friend of 15 years: "I liked to listen to Jack sing. He would do songs like *Stars Fell On Alabama, After You've Gone, Basin Street Blues,* and my favorite, *A Hundred Years from Today.* He was very much like Louis and Bing.....always liked to sing the songs he played well and I would back him up on my big bass." Since the loss of Teagarden and Armstrong, Arvell began singing during gigs which started in Oslo, Norway, when one of the musicians bet he wouldn't sing during his featured spot: "I sang *St. James Infirmary,* the only song I knew the lyrics to. I thought of Jack a lot that night, and Louis rolled up his eyes at me."

In the movie *Birth of the Blues* with Bing in 1941, Jack was at his sterling best as both player and jazz vocalist. He collaborated with Mary Martin and Bing Crosby singing Johnny Mercer's tune *The Waiter and the Porter and The Upstairs Maid.*

Jack Teagarden retained his full playing and singing powers until the end of his life in his beloved New Orleans in 1964.

CAB CALLOWAY—The Hi-De-Hi-De-Ho Man.

After nixing an offer to play basketball with the Harlem Globetrotters, Cab Calloway hustled his way through the Roaring Twenties and right into The Cotton Club where he made his indelible mark. "We played in the Cotton Club whenever Duke had a "gig" somewhere else," he said in his autobiography. When he sang in a white zoot suit, his presence on stage was electric. He'd sing, "Hi-de-hi-de-ho," and the

**Hi-De-Ho-Man Cab Calloway. Even his smile was energetic.
(Richard Grudens Collection)**

audience answered, "Wah-de-do-de-way-do-ho," that started accidentally when Cab forgot the words while on a radio show and began scatting the lyrics. Calloway made his fans forget the Great Depression with his singing, stomping and dancing.

"In the simplest terms," Cab said, "we were raising hell in those days. We were in and out of the movies, making records, smashing attendance records everywhere, and doing national radio shows. Lord, were we riding high., beginning with Jolson's *The Singing Kid.* We did about ten films, too."

Tall and slender with hair waving from side to side, he punched out songs like *Minnie the Moocher,* who became a household name. "Since 1931, when I wrote *Minnie,* I've written more than a hundred tunes, some of them alone, often out of my own loneliness, and a few of them with others. I don't need to add that none of them has ever been as important to me as *Minnie,* though I have had fun with many of them." Calloway worked and played with Louis Armstrong, Lena Horne, Duke Ellington, Al Jolson, Dizzy Gillespie and Bill "Bojangles" Robinson. Cab Calloway knew how to entertain and make people happy.

In 1937, when the Cotton Club closed, Cab Calloway took his band on the road for an extended tour. Records were broken at the New York Paramount, the Meadowbrook supper club in Cedar Grove, New Jersey, and the Cocoanut Grove and Zanzibar Club in Manhattan.

In 1967, at the age of sixty, Cab did a Broadway show opposite Pearl Bailey in *Hello, Dolly!*

Some of Cab's jive talk that appears in his constantly updated Hipsters Dictionary, and words like *apple* (the big town), *canary* (girl vocalist), *cat* (musician in a swing band), *Armstrong's* (upper register, high trumpet notes), "gimme some skin" (shake hands), *the Man* (the law), are lasting colloquialisms we have absorbed over the years. Cab Calloway was one of the great singing bandleaders who helped shaped the Big Band Era.

In the 1950's when I worked at NBC, I knew a song writer named J. Fred Coots who wrote *Santa Claus is Coming to Town* and *For All We Know*. Fred and I would talk for hours about his role writing songs (with Benny Davis) for Cab Calloway and the *Cotton Club Parade* shows. "We were so busy we hardly had time to breathe," he once told me, "Cab was an honest-to-goodness super entertainer. It was a joy to write songs after the tradition of Harold Arlen and Ted Koehler (who wrote *Stormy Weather* for the Cotton Club). Cab loved good music, fast horses, a game of cards and a bottle of whiskey, a few close friends, and most of all, life itself. Working with him was the most exciting time of my life."

Sadly for us, on November 18, 1994, an 86 year old Cab passed away.

JIMMY RUSHING—Mr. Five by Five.

This great Basie Band blues-singing soloist was a most distinctive individual. His generous body and his powerful voice were standards of the 1930's Basie organization. Born James Andrew Rushing in 1902, both his parents were musicians. His father was a trumpet player in a brass band, and his mother a church singer, so James studied music theory in Douglas High School in Oklahoma City and Wilberforce University in Ohio. His Uncle Wesley taught him how to sing the blues. Migrating to the West Coast, he played parties with Jelly Roll Morton and was a singing waiter in night clubs. In 1925 he toured with the great Walter Page's Blue Devils, making his first records in 1928 and 1929.

Rushing's prolific career spanned Bennie Moten's and Basie's great locomotive band that was working the Reno Club in Kansas City. "Jimmy's enthusiasm and optimism kept our boys going even when the going got rough on those tough days on the road," Basie told me back in the 1980's during an interview. The recording *Boogie-Woogie* (also called *I May Be Wrong*) became long-standing Rushing-Basie standards.

Back in those days there were no microphones. "You had to have a good pair of lungs to be heard," Jimmy was once quoted as saying.

In 1950, when Basie broke up his first band, Jimmy tried retiring, but couldn't take the quiet life: "The first time a band came through town I'd be finished. It happened and I told my wife we were packing our bags and going back to New York." In his own band he recorded *Goin' To Chicago* (a Joe Williams favorite) in an album *Jimmy Rushing Sings The Blues,* accompanying himself on piano. His players were Walter Page, Jo Jones,and Buddy Tate, all Basie sidemen. Jimmy reunited with Count Basie in 1957 with Lester Young and Jo Jones at the Newport Jazz Festival, the tracks of the festival released later on Verve recordings. In 1962, he recorded with Earl Hines Band and my friend Budd Johnson on *Gee Baby, Ain't I Good to You* and *Who Was It Sang That Song.* Jimmy Rushing admired most the singers Ethel Waters, Perry Como, Bing Crosby, and Louis Armstrong, "You see," he said, "I love music and I love singing it." We lost Jimmy Rushing in 1972. Joe Williams has valiantly carried the torch for that kind of blues singing ever since. Both Basie and Budd Johnson told me they very much admired the work of Jimmy Rushing.

**Thomas "Fats" Waller on the set of the film *Stormy Weather*, 1943.
(Richard Grudens Collection)**

FATS WALLER—Lived Hard, Died Young.

Most everybody loved Thomas Fats Waller, whose songs were mostly cheerful and definitely unforgettable, effervescent and energetic. Born Thomas Wright Waller on May 21, 1904 in New York City, he began as a piano player for the Fletcher Henderson Orchestra when he was only twenty-three, although he started playing professionally at the age of fifteen even though his father, a clergyman, tried to stop him.

A black musician in a white-dominated industry, his was a story of hard struggles of a once serious piano stylist. I recall Red Norvo telling me recently that while married to Mildred Bailey and living in Forest Hills on Long Island, Fats Waller used to go over to their house along with people like blues singer Bessie Smith, vocalist Lee Wiley, and bandleader Bunny Berigan, "and play and sing and eat like crazy. We were all good friends. Fats was well-known then,"he said. Actually Fats Waller was one of the few outstanding jazz musicians to achieve wide commercial fame during his lifetime. He obscured his great musical talents under a guise of a singing comedian. From 1934 on he recorded dozens of records with his own band, mixed with both slapstick and charm.

Waller was influenced by James P. Johnson, who found the stride school of jazz piano.

Waller wrote lots of great songs: *Ain't Misbehavin', I've Got a Feeling I'm Falling, Honeysuckle Rose, What Did I Do To Be So Black and Blue, Prisoner of Love, Heart of Stone, Blue Velvet,* and *Squeeze Me* (his first success), are just a few, most of which he personally recorded and sang publicly, employing his own original brand of ingenious clowning. His son, Maurice Waller, collaborated with Anthony Calabrese on his biography, *Fats Waller,* in 1977.

RUSS COLUMBO—A Career Cut Short.

Bing Crosby once spoke about his rival Russ Columbo, the *Prisoner of Love* recording star: "I worked with Russ in 1930 at the Cocoanut Grove. We were in the Gus Arnheim band together. He played violin (and accordion) and sang. I just sang. I am sure if Russ had lived (longer), he would have been a big, big star. A talented, fine musician, he was a most attractive and appealing fellow." His similar crooning is

Early crooner Russ Columbo in the 1930's.
(Richard Grudens Collection)

sometimes mistaken for Bing's. Appearances at the Cocoanut Grove catapulted both Crosby and Columbo's careers.

In 1931 Ruggiero de Rudolpho Columbo formed his own band and became a sensation with a very silky, ballad style of singing, suggesting him as a Bing Crosby rival. One of the songs that heralded him was his own composition *You Call It Madness* (but, I call it love). Columbo toured the U.S. and Europe singing *Prisoner of Love, Paradise, Auf Wiedersehen,* and *Too Beautiful for Words,* among others. Columbo made a few films: *Moulin Rouge, Wake Up and Dream, The Street Girl,* and *Broadway Through a Keyhole.* He also recorded with Jimmie Grier's orchestra. His exciting, promising career came to a sudden end in a bizarre accident. On September 2, 1934, a photographer friend was showing him an old pair of dueling pistols and struck a match to one of them that, unbeknown to anyone, turned out to be loaded. Russ Columbo was hit in the head by a ricocheting bullet.

PHIL HARRIS—Hi, Ya, Jackson!

Phil Harris, the fast-drawling band leader, radio's sidekick to Jack Benny and golf and hunting cohort of Bing Crosby, wasn't really a singer. Or was he? His songs were down-home, country bumpkin kind of sounds. He came off as a wise-guy, prompting his boss Jack Benny to say, "It's hard to explain. Phil is a typical fresh guy found in every town. For some reason or another people seem to love that type of fellow."

That's What I Like About the South, Is It True What They Say About Dixie, Smoke, Smoke, That Cigarette, and his big hit *The Thing* were the kinds of tunes Phil Harris sang and recorded. For seventeen years Phil played one-night stands, sleeping in buses. "I never voted," he once said, "because I never had a residence."

Growing up in Nashville, Tennessee, Phil played the drums—not the guitar, as you would think in such a town. His father was a circus bandmaster and vaudeville musician who hired his own son at the age of six. Phil's first band was called the Dixie Syncopaters. The band toured for two years. Later, his newly-formed orchestra moved into radio, landing him a permanent spot on Jack Benny's popular radio program, which led to parts in movies including a role in the 1954 film *The High and the Mighty.* His rendition of *The Bare Necessities* in the Disney cartoon film *The Jungle Book,* garnered him an Academy Award nomination.

I loved Phil Harris' wise-guy character and his salty vocals. Married for years to the lovely actress/singer Alice Faye, Phil Harris passed from us in 1995 at the age of 91. He's probably up there right now giving St.Peter a hard time and calling him "Pete."

**A rare Frank Sinatra Waldorf-Astoria menu cover from the late 1940's.
(Jack Ellsworth Collection)**

FRANK SINATRA

One of the Hoboken Four Goes Solo

For over half a century Frank Sinatra has sung his heart out while the world listened. In my diligent search for the most prolific recording artist of our lifetime, I turned every stone but could not make the needed connection. I turned to Susan Reynolds of Scoop Marketing in Los Angeles who represents Frank Sinatra these days. Regretfully, Susan was duty-bound to deny us the access we coveted, although she honestly tried.

She wrote: "As you may be aware, Mr. Sinatra is taking time off after more than 50 years performing concerts throughout the world. He appreciates your kind invitation to participate in the upcoming book *The Music Men*, but he is not taking on additional projects and is thus not available."

Frank is on a kind of health-hiatus, and, realizing no book about singers is much of a book without him, we proceeded without the benefit of a direct interview. Instead, we talked to those who knew and worked with him over the years, thus compiling a composite of anecdotes and facts from previous interviews and declarations.

Almost everyone knows *the* Frank Sinatra story. Presented on film and a subject of many books authorized and unauthorized, Frank's turbulent life has been a virtual open book. His daughter, Nancy, has produced some remarkable coffee table books about his career, as well, with endless photos.

My friend, best-known and best-loved disc jockey William B. Williams, long time host of the *Make Believe Ballroom* radio program on New York's WNEW, was a great friend of Frank Sinatra. It was William B. (as he was affectionately known) who coined the Sinatra sobriquet *Chairman of the Board*, which Frank, himself admitted he always tried to live up to. In 1984, William B., who consistently said, "I don't care how a record sells, just how it sounds," held a rare interview with Frank, and sent me a now treasured copy of the tape which began,

"Hello, World! This is William B. and I'd like to introduce you to Francis Albert Sinatra, a practically unknown singer. Say something, Francis, don't be shy!"

"Hello, (he chuckles) World, this is Francis Albert Sinatra. You know, Willy B., about 40 years ago I started at WNEW, and do you know what I got paid—zilch—*but*—they gave me thirty-five cents in carfare to get back to New Jersey. Well, I'm back again for those of you who ever wondered what happened to me. I know they're still paying the same kind of bread which may explain why William B. has been able to keep his job here."

A little before that, in 1935, a guy named Major Bowes fronted a show called *The Amateur Hour,* where many talented performers got their start. One night the Major introduced a new group:

"Good evening friends, we start the dizzy spin of the wheel of fortune—around and round she goes and where she stops nobody knows," the Major said in his gravelly eloquence, "Now, first four youngsters in kinda nice suits—*The Hoboken Four.* They seem so happy, I guess, and they seem to make everybody else happy (gentle laughter from the audience). Tell me, where do you work in Hoboken?"

"I'm Frank, Major. We're looking for jobs. How about it! (more appreciative laughter from the audience to Frank's good-natured boldness) Everyone that's ever heard us—liked us. We think we're pretty good."

"All right, what do you want to sing—or dance—or whatever it is you do?"

"We're gonna sing *Shine* and then we're gonna dance."

"All right! Let's have it!", the Major announced, "... here's *The Hoboken Four.*" They closely emulated a Bing Crosby-Mills Brothers version of the then popular song.

It was a very slim-looking Frank Sinatra's first public appearance into the world of performing that would last some 62 musically eventful years. The Hoboken Four toured with the Amateur Hour Show, earning seventy-five dollars a week.

"We were getting paid, we were no longer amateurs," said Frank.

Let's jump ahead some 10 years to 1945...some things have changed. Frank was singing to thousands of screaming bobby soxers at New York's Paramount Theater with the great bands of Harry James and, later, Tommy Dorsey. Were you one of those screaming youngsters?

In 1981, while interviewing Johnny Mince, Tommy Dorsey's clarinet player, he talked about first seeing Sinatra: "We were ready to go on a one-nighter, and Tommy says, 'C-mere John.' He took me across the street and they had it on the juke-box—that thing he did with Harry James—*All or Nothing at All.* I says, 'Boy this guy is good!' his voice rising. But my first impression meeting Frank, he was such a skinny, beat-up looking guy, compared to Jack Leonard (the singer who just left) who had lots of class and was good-looking. Of course, Frank sure turned out to be a great one."

During my interview with Harry James in 1981, he said exactly this: "At that time Frank considered himself the greatest vocalist in the business. Get that! No one ever heard of him. He never had a hit record. He looks like a wet rag. But he tells me he's the greatest. He believed. And you know what, he was right." By this time Frank was now out on his own as a single and the screams and carrying on continued wherever he appeared. "Kiss me once and kiss me twice and kiss me once again....It's been a long, long time...." Frank's way of embracing a microphone with a new approach to putting over a song, completely won over a fast-growing female audience. He copied Bing Crosby and he absorbed Billie Holiday's way of bending a tune.

With both Harry James and Tommy Dorsey, Frank was the boy singer and Connie Haines was the girl singer; "I was just eighteen, and I remember the police escorting Frank and me across the street from the Paramount Theater over to the Astor Hotel, through the lobby into the drugstore just to get a hamburger, "Connie and I have frequent conversations about the "history of our kind of music," as she succinctly puts it. "We could not get away from the screaming kids even to eat." Connie remembered some early enthusiasm three years before when they both sang with Harry James. "Richard, it was something about the way he'd hang on to that microphone. Something in his singing that reached out to the audience—like he was saying, 'I'm giving this to you with every-

69

FRANK SINATRA

April 15, 1997

Dear Jack,

We've traveled many musical miles
together, my friend. I am delighted
to send cheers and bravos to you
on 50 marvelous years of championing
our kind of music.

As I raise a glass of bubbly, I thank
you for your generous support of my
career -- you're a good man!

Frank Sinatra

Mr. Jack Ellsworth
WLIM Radio
Woodside Avenue
Patchogue, N.Y. 11772

A letter to Jack Ellsworth from Frank Sinatra. Jack owns one of the biggest collections of Sinatra recordings. (Jack Ellsworth Collection)

thing I've got; what have you got to give me?' I guess they came back-stage afterwards to tell him.

"Frank and I didn't always get along in those days, but, Frank showed his true colors one night—even though we were feuding while we sang songs like *Let's Get Away from It All, Oh, Look at Me Now,* and *Snootie Little Cutie*—when my dress caught fire because someone tossed a lit cigarette down from the balcony and it got snared in my dress netting. Tommy was still vamping, not aware of what was happening. Frank reacted quickly, throwing his suit jacket over me and flinging me to the ground, snuffing out the flames—probably saving my life."

When Sinatra joined up with Tommy Dorsey, Jo Stafford was the lead singer of the Pied Pipers singing group: "Frank made a special effort to get a good blend with the Pipers. Most solo singers usually don't fit too well into a group, but Frank never stopped working at it and, of course, as you know, he blended beautifully with us. He was meticulous about his phrasing and dynamics. He worked very hard so that his vibrato would match ours. And he was always conscientious about learning his parts. The first song I ever heard him sing was *Stardust.* I thought, wow, this guy is destined for great success as a singer."

Gene Lees, in his book *Singers and the Song,* records Frank Sinatra as the best singer he had ever heard and one of the best singers in history. "Sinatra learned breath control from Tommy Dorsey's technique of slowly and deliberately releasing air to support long lyrical melodic lines and was indeed instructive to Sinatra. Dorsey would use this control to tie the end of one phrase into the start of the next. Sinatra learned to do the same."

Sinatra's first recordings with Columbia Records exposed the public to a band singer who no longer sang songs to which you could only dance. Axel Stordahl was his arranger, helped too, by George Siravo. Frank was just twenty-six and Stordahl about the same. They produced some classic Sinatra sides together, with music that had some imagination and gutty arrangements. Remember *Dream, The Girl That I Marry, Put Your Dreams Away, Day by Day?*

At the end of the 1940's Frank Sinatra's career changed. He rebelled against Columbia's chief, Mitch Miller, who was producing his own kind of music which bothered him and which he thought demeaned his skills as a singer.

Rosemary Clooney loved Frank Sinatra. Manie Sacks, A&R man at Columbia and later one of my friends at NBC, answered Sinatra's request for a girl singer by suggesting Rosemary. Frank said OK. "We did two sides of that first date together, but later on we did some other things. That first session was the thrill of my life because I had always been such a Sinatra fan. I loved him when I was in high school, and it was great working with him. He kept up the quality in every recording date."

By 1952 Frank Sinatra was without a movie contract, recording contract, or management. Because of those late 1940's forty-five to fifty shows a week, which meant 100 songs a day, the great voice tired, his personal life tumbling into a shambles. But, he promptly started on the road back to even greater success, propelled by his acting-only role in the movie *From Here To Eternity,* his move from Columbia to Johnny Mercer's Capitol Records, and his union with master arranger Nelson Riddle. Nelson taught Frank how to "swing." Their first album together was, what else, *Swing Easy,* followed by *Songs for Young Lovers* (Nelson and George Siravo) and *In the Wee Small Hours of the Morning,* literally revising his career. He proceeded to record over twenty albums from 1953 to 1961, all hits. The songs: *Just One of Those Things, My Funny Valentine, A Foggy Day, Last Night When We Were Young, This Love of Mine* (he co-wrote this one), *What Is This Thing Called Love.*

"I first met Frank Sinatra when he was with Tommy Dorsey," said Duke Ellington in 1973, "They all came down one night at the College Inn at the Sherman Hotel in Chicago where we were playing, about the time he was ready to split the Dorsey gig. I could tell that by the way Tommy said *good night* to him. He was young, crispy-crunch fresh, and the girls were squealing then. He was easy to get along with, and there were no hassles about his music. Every song he sings is understandable and, most of all, believable, which is the ultimate in theater. And I must repeat and emphasize my admiration for him as a nonconformist. When he played the Paramount the chicks were screaming. He was an individualist, nobody tells him what to do or say."

In the late 1960's both Sinatra and Ellington were playing Las Vegas, and Frank was having a birthday party. Ellington asked permission from the management to go over and play a few numbers for Frank. They did and they had a ball," I thanked Frank for the great time and told him it was the best party he ever gave for Paul Gonsalves (Ellington sideman), who had such a great time he had to be carried out bodily."

"In 1961 my father asked Morris "Mo" Ostin, who was with Verve Records, to head up his own label, Reprise, "said daughter, Nancy," It was very important for Dad to have his own recording company."

According to Frank himself, "I always like to choose my own songs for an album.....to keep all the songs in the same genre'—swing, love songs, etc. Once I decide what type of music I want, I make up a list of song titles, and my associates—arrangers—suggest songs. When we actually get down to where arrangements have to be done, I go through the list again and pick out eight to ten songs and go with them." The first Reprise selections: *A Foggy Day, A Fine Romance, Be Careful, It's My Heart.*

When I talked with legendary jazz vibraphonist Red Norvo recently, he championed Frank as a great singer: "We worked together in Vegas and then at the Fountainbleu in Florida and also in Atlantic City. We also went to Australia. I was used to handling singers in my various bands (Red Norvo was married to the first regular big band girl singer Mildred Bailey and is a recognized jazz master), so Frank was never a problem to me. When we first worked together, I had a trio, which was too small, so I told him we needed a drummer and sax, and he said OK. We made a couple of movies: *Kings Go Forth,* where I wrote some of the music, and *Oceans 11,* a kinda funny movie where Frank plays a bank robber in Vegas. Our Capitol recordings of the late sixties are just being issued now. Heard they are number four on the charts. Isn't that sumthin'?"

Frank Sinatra continued his singing activities until he announced retirement in 1971. There were loud signals when Frank poured out albums like *Cycles, A Man Alone,* and the closer *My Way,* in the late sixties. He returned gradually doing some concerts into 1973 and producing an album, *Old Blue Eyes Is Back,* arranged by Gordon Jenkins and Don Costa. The songs: *Send in the Clowns, You Will Be My Music.* Frank toured triumphantly with Woody Herman in 1974 and spawned the album *The Main Event.* The songs: *The Lady Is a Tramp, I Get a Kick Out of You, Autumn in New York, My Kind of Town, My Way.*

1975 produced a series of appearances at the Uris Theater in New York and then London with the great band of Count Basie which included the presence of the divine Sarah Vaughan.

In the eighties, Quincy Jones' talents became linked to Frank Sinatra's musical life, beginning with the album *L.A. is My Lady.* "Frank is remarkable. When we recorded at A & M's studios in New York, I called the orchestra for three hours before. We rehearsed and set the balance. Frank came in at seven o'clock and so help me God, at eight-twenty he went home We had done four songs," he said. The songs: *Stormy Weather, How Do You Keep the Music Playing, After You've Gone.*

My favorite Sinatra recording is an early swinging gem, *Sweet Lorraine,* a perfect blend of voice and instrument. It features jazz all-stars

Nat King Cole on piano, Johnny Hodges on alto sax, Charlie Shavers on trumpet, Coleman Hawkins on tenor sax, and Eddie Safranki (one of my old NBC buddies), on bass. Amazing group. Perfect recording.

Frank Sinatra made many films, but didn't sing in all of them. We'll leave that for film writers to ponder.

Once, appearing with William B. Williams at WNEW on the *Make Believe Ballroom Show,* Frank had a speaking part: "Hi there, my name is Francis Albert Sinatra and I've got news for you. Here is your host, William B. Williams."

"Name dropper!" William B. answered tongue-in-cheek, "A question, Francis, that is somewhat philosophic. I know how keenly you feel about your family and your two granddaughters. The legacy that you leave them, is there any particular way you want to be remembered as a man...as a performer...as an American...as a human being?"

"Well, Willy, I realize it's a broad question, but I can narrow it by saying that I'd like to be remembered as a man who was as honest as he knew how to be in his life and as honest as he knew how to be in his work...and a man who gave as much energy in what he did every day as anybody else ever did. I'd like to be remembered as a decent father, as a fair husband, and as a great granddad...wonderful grandpop. And I'd like to be remembered as a good friend to my friends."

I think the only addendum I would add is...as a man who *enjoyed.*"

"Ah! That's true. I didn't want to get into that because, you know, there's an old 14th century Spanish adage....'living well is the best revenge'...If that applied to anybody, it must apply to me." Frank was also being philosophical.

"I knew many men like that. in my lifetime....a guy named Errol Flynn...John Barrymore, even (Humphrey) Bogart. All those great men who are now gone—they came to play. That lifestyle is almost gone now. People like Rubirosa and other men I met around New York through the years. People like Toots Shor—it's nearly gone now. I assume I may be one of the last of that kind. I think that's what we're here for...to make the best of every day, to get the most out of every day...and I worked like Hell to do that, too."

Frank Sinatra has always worked for the benefit of those in need. Helen O'Connell told me that Frank secretly paid all the medical bills for fellow singer Bob Eberly.

William B. once told me about Frank's great work that gathered millions for Sloan-Kettering Memorial Cancer Hospital in New York. At the 67th Street out-patient entrance between York and 1st Avenues of that hospital there is a plaque on the wall that states "This Wing of Sloan-Kettering is Through the Efforts of Frank Sinatra."

Today, Frank and Barbara Sinatra work hard for Barbara Sinatra Children's Center at Eisenhower Center, Rancho Mirage, California. Profits from their new book, *The Sinatra Celebrity Cookbook* by Barbara, Frank & Friends, support that project.

That's about all I have to say about *the* Big Band singer, Frank Sinatra, although it would be easy enough to create volumes about just his singing alone.

**Sheet music of *A Lovely Way To Spend An Evening*, 1940's.
(Photo–Movie Star News)**

**A very youthful Mel Tormé when he acted in radio soap operas.
(Richard Grudens Collection)**

MEL TORMÉ

"I was all over the place."

I've been chasing Mel Tormé for years. In 1984, in a town named Port Jefferson, on Long Island, along with cornetist Dick Sudhalter, singer and pianist Daryl Sherman and bassist supreme Jay Leonhart, Mel and I were supposed to talk about his life for the show business tabloid *Long Island PM*. Everyone showed up but Mel didn't make it. At the 1995 Long Island Jazz Festival, run by a lady friend Teddy Bookman of Friends of the Arts, Mel showed up all right and dished up a terrific show—and I mean a *terrific* show, but I arrived too late for a pre-show interview, and due to the show's running over and Mel's firing up an appreciative crowd with encores, no interview could be granted after the show. It was simple greetings and hasty farewells. The tour had to catch a plane for the next gig.

Mel Torme first impressed me in the bright, happy MGM collegiate film *Good News,* with lovely June Allyson and Peter Lawford (who sang *Be a Ladies Man* with Mel). Mel crooned through the title song as well as *Be a Ladies Man,* showing off his impressive singing talents for the first time on screen. In his book, the 1967 version of *The Big Bands,* George Simon noted that in 1946 Artie Shaw began featuring some quality singing on his new label called Musicraft Records. "Back came the strings, and in came some exceptionally good singers, Kitty Kallen and a young Chicagoan and his vocal group, Mel Torme and the Meltones, who provided some brilliant singing on some Cole Porter tunes, *Get Out of Town* and *What is This Thing Called Love.*"

So, who is this actor/song writer/arranger/ drummer/innovative jazz singer, dancer, and musical director Mel Tormé? Let me tell you a little about this very fascinating guy: Mel actually started as a child of four singing solo with the then world-famous Coon-Sanders Orchestra on a *coast-to-coast* radio show originating from the Blackhawk Restaurant in Chicago. "An important band, it was really like—well—Benny Goodman—an amazingly popular big-name for the time," Mel told veteran broadcaster and author Fred Hall a few years back."It was 1929. I loved radio—you see, for me, radio was more fascinating than my set of Lionel trains."

The first song Mel ever sang in public was *You're Drivin' Me Crazy* with the Coon-Sanders Orchestra. Later he sang it with the Buddy Rogers band at the College Inn in the Hotel Sherman, which became a regular gig for Mel. "That song finally became a hit for me in 1947," Mel said.

Over the years Mel kinda sneaked up on the public. In 1949, for instance, Bing Crosby had a big hit with *Dear Hearts and Gentle People,* my friend Frankie Laine sold big with *Mule Train,* and Mel scored high with *Careless Hands.* But, *Careless Hands* was not as big or as nationally accepted as the recordings of the more established Crosby and Laine. These guys were scoring hit after hit, year after year, and Mel was a comparatively new voice, although he had an earlier hit with a very smooth rendition of Rogers and Hart's *Blue Moon,* a recording which earned him the sobriquet "The Velvet Fog." My colleague Mike Prelee, host of New Jersey's WVNJ radio show *In The Spotlight,* said to Mel in late 1996, in perhaps one of Mel's last interviews before he fell ill: "I heard you didn't like being called 'The Velvet Fog.'"

Chuckling, Mel said, "Freddie Robbins (famous disc jockey) gave me that back in 1947. It stuck like glue, so I kinda came to grips with it. I don't mind it now because a lot of older people come up to me and say, 'Gee, I grew up with you and we loved your records and, of course, you are "The Velvet Fog" to us.' So, I suddenly took a look at myself and I thought—why am I being so abrasive? It's not terrible—and it *is* descriptive—it's not how I sing now, I mean I am no more "The Velvet Fog" now than Frank Sinatra. I used to sing in that creamy, soft way, and so I have gotten to the point now where my license plates on my car say *Le Phog,*" he laughs heartily.

At one time Capitol Records thought that Mel would replace Frank Sinatra after Frank's career began nose-diving at the dawn of the rock and roll era. But Mel was a jazz singer and not accustomed to being instructed what to sing and how to sing it, so it didn't work out. Instead,

**Mel Tormé and Radio's Mike Prelee taken after an interview on Mike's
WVNJ *In The Spotlight* show in late 1996. (Mike Prelee Collection)**

he moved on to record albums with fellow arranger Marty Paich, particularly on a 1960 album *Mel Tormé Swings Shubert Alley.*

Here's the Tormé story: Mel was first a drummer: "I was a drum-
and-bugle corps kid in grammar school. I loved Chick Webb and, obvi-
ously, Gene Krupa," Mel told Fred Hall, "and finally, Buddy Rich.
Those are the people who motivated me as a young man." Then, an
actor: "I was a child radio actor, probably one of the five busiest child
actors in America, from 1933 to 1941." Mel did *Mary Noble, Backstage
Wife; Captain Midnight; Little Orphan Annie;* and even *Jack Armstrong*
radio shows. Next, a songwriter and vocal group arranger very influenced by the fact that Frank Sinatra broke away from Tommy Dorsey's
orchestra and went on his own as a solo vocalist. "I could see the writing on the wall," he said, "and since I was a singer, I just followed the
path of least resistance. And look what's happened to me. I mean, my
God, look at me: I've become a singer!"

Quintessential musician: Besides drums, he plays a four string guitar and piano. As a songwriter, *A Lament To Love,* his first song written at age fourteen, was eventually recorded by Harry James. Mel was still in high school.

Author: In addition to writing non-fiction articles about gun-collecting, motion pictures, World War I aviation, and sports cars, Mel has written both fiction and biographical books. Among them a semi-factual Western called *Dollarhide* (under the pseudonym Wesley Wyatt), which was later re-written for *The Virginian* television show; *The Other Side of the Rainbow,* about working the Judy Garland television show during a frenetic nine-month period; his own autobiographical *It Wasn't All Velvet;* a portrait of his good friend, big band drummer Buddy Rich, *Trapps, The Drum Wonder,* done as a last wish by Buddy to Mel, and more recently, *My Singing Teachers,* reflections on a lifetime of listening and learning to all the greats who influenced his life. Whew! Mel works very hard.

Influences: His earliest days were captured by the imagination of Duke Ellington. The Ellington touch was home base. "You gotta understand," Mel said, "I was a Duke Ellington idolater. I mean, there are not *words.* I can't describe what I felt for Duke Ellington—on a personal as well as a professional plane." Mel was also struck by Bing Crosby and Ella Fitzgerald, "those two vocalists more than everyone else—moved me—put their hands in the small of my back and said...'Go!' Nobody comes close to Ella—I miss her. Bing—well—he was the singer of the century, the man who started all of us," Mel said back in 1994, when he was performing at Michael's Pub in Manhattan.

As arranger & musical director: "Let's talk about the Mel-Tones. It only lasted four years," Mel noted, "but we did a lot in that time. Aside from recording with Artie Shaw, we sang everything, everywhere. If anybody wanted to hear singing, we'd be there to sing for them. It was during the War—we went to the Hollywood Canteen and sang there endlessly—also traveled to many camps all over the map." Mel's Mel-Tones performed brilliantly on *White Christmas, What is This Thing Called Love,* with Artie Shaw, *Day by Day,* with Bing Crosby (who was a Mel Tormé admirer), and *Am I Blue,* among others.

As a (jazz) vocalist: "When I recorded *Again, Blue Moon* was on the back side. After *Again* ran its course, *Blue Moon's* success was astonishing to me—I was knocked out by it—Pete Rugolo (the arranger) was a big help." With the *event* of the *Lulu's Back in Town* recording, Mel Torme left the crooning business: "I was kinda a crooner before that—now I sounded like an instrument. I went to Bethlehem Records and first put out *Lulu,* the audience said, 'Hey this guy can sing jazz.'"

Mel always prefers performing live, saying it brings out the very best in a performer. "You got to do it *right* and *now*. You're not going to get another chance—like in a studio where you can stop and fix the tape—you are live—that's the challenge."

When I finally reached Mel Tormé, he wrapped up his life's philosophy for me: "I'm proud of achieving, more than anything. When you stand in front of a great symphony orchestra—like the Boston Pops— and they're playing the notes I put down on paper, it's the closest thing to being God-like. I think, 'those people are playing my music.' As for retiring—if you rest, you rust. When I look around and find it's not fun anymore, then I'll quit. But, right now I'm having too much fun singing."

At this writing, Mel Tormé is marking time in his living room. Struck down by a stroke in August of 1996, while in the studio doing a tribute to Ella for a CD, Mel had to quit performing. By Christmas a respiratory infection set in, but doctors say his long-term outlook is good. He's definitely a fighter, receiving daily physical, occupational and speech therapy.

Speaking to Mel's manager, Dale Sheets, today, January 10, 1998, Dale offered this piece of information regarding Mel Tormé. "He's back home recuperating and working on returning to singing once again. He still has a while to go. I guess it was worse than we first thought. We're keeping him down a bit. But, Mel's not a guy to stay put for too long."

I recall Mel's closing words of his autobiography: "Early on, it certainly wasn't *all* velvet. Now the fog has lifted."

The Velvet Fog *will* be back!

Tony Martin's song sheet of Richard Whiting's *When Did You Leave Heaven* from the movie *Sing, Baby, Sing,* 1946. (Richard Grudens Collection)

TONY MARTIN

It Was Written In The Stars Just For Him.

On a very hot summer day this past July, Music Man Tony Martin and I sat down to talk about his phenomenal career at the very cool Regency Hotel in New York. Tony had just flown in from his Los Angeles home to appear at Carnegie Hall the following Tuesday night along with a company of fellow MGM musical stars celebrating their tenure with the Culver City dream factory in a fitting tribute. Performers scheduled were June Allyson, Betty Garrett, Dolores Gray, Betty Comden, Adolph Green, Julie Wilson, Celeste Holm, Mickey Rooney, Cyd Charisse, Ann Miller, Leslie Caron, Arlene Dahl, Gloria De Haven, Roddy McDowell, Van Johnson, Donald O'Connor, and Kathryn Grayson. The host would be cabaret singer favorite Michael Feinstein.

"I started out my professional life as an Oakland (California) newsboy with my given name Alvin Morris, and learned to play tenor sax. When I became good enough I joined a band," Tony said proudly with the intonation of a forty year old—clear, rich and succinct. Tony worked in a number of big bands including Bob Crosby's, Ray McKinley's, and the Glenn Miller Army Air Force Band: "I actually learned to sing by mistake. I was playing in the band and the regular singer took sick." Famous columnist Walter Winchell, who had a popular radio show in those days called *The Magic Carpet* featuring name bands, heard about Tony's singing. "I got up and did a song—you know—took a shot at it—and Winchell wanted to know 'who was that singer?'—and it was me!"

Tony's first big band recording was with Ray Noble's band. "*I Hadn't Anyone Till You* was a very popular song...I was always lucky with good songs," Tony said, "I also worked in the Anson Weeks band in those days. I sang on Anson's night off—I knew him pretty well—I replaced the sax player and didn't sing regularly."

83

Tony claims that luck had a lot to do with his success. "Again, I joined a band led by Tom Guerin, the same day as Woody Herman did—and we worked Sunday nights. We were the only band on because the big hotels were closed on Sunday—you know—no dancin'—but we worked the Bell Tavern in San Francisco and the program went down to LA and was heard at a party held at L.B. Mayer's (Metro-Goldwyn-Mayer film studio boss) house in Malibu and they heard me sing *Poor Butterfly,* which was a very popular song then. Now that was the kind of luck I was experiencing at the time." Tony was quickly located by an agent sent by Mayer and was invited to do a screen test. That led to Tony's first films, *Sing, Baby, Sing* and *Follow the Fleet* in 1936 with Fred Astaire and two other hopefuls, Lucille Ball and Betty Grable.

"Where did the name Tony Martin come from?" I asked.

"Well, after the screen test, the people there said there were too many Morris's at Universal. There were (actors) Chester Morris and Wayne Morris, and I was Alvin Morris. They were concerned about the three of us possibly being cast in the same movie. So I took the name from band leader Freddy Martin who was playing at the Cocoanut Grove nightclub in 1936. I was out on a date and the girl I was dancing with suggested that *Martin* would work best for me and I thought that was pretty good—I liked it. Anthony—which, of course, becomes Tony, came from a fellow I knew in Maryland who liked to gamble on house-boats, so I took that name, which I thought was an exciting name and put them together. So it was Tony Martin!"

"When people talk about you they invariably recall your role as Pepe LeMoko, the movie character you played in *Casbah,*" I said, "It was a very popular movie with some great songs by (composer) Harold Arlen. That movie certainly impressed me as a youngster."

"Oh, yes! Well, I experience the same thing...when I'm in a restaurant or if I'm shopping in a store.....and it's a good feeling. It was a good movie with Yvonne DeCarlo, who was a very good dancer, and Peter Lorre. We filmed it mostly on the backlots at Universal—and we also went to Algiers for a couple of scenes." (Tony enthusiastically sings out *a capella*—"Love-love—hoo-ray for love.......It was writ-ten in the star-r-r-s........What's go-o-od ab-out good-bye-e-e...," portions of three of the movies top songs—*Hooray for Love, It Was Written In the Stars,* and *What's Good About Goodbye?*)

Tony Martin, lyricist Leo Robin and Harold Arlen rehearse the song *For Every Man There's A Woman* **for the film** *Casbah.* **(Sam Arlen Collection)**

"Harold Arlen wrote a great score (Leo Robin wrote the words) and it was his last movie score—and he interpreted each of the songs by singing them *to* me....*for* me. We'd sit at the piano and we'd sing each song—first him—then I would take a turn. Harold was articulate, a fantastic dresser—a very nice man who always wore a flower on his lapel. I recorded 14 of his songs. I love best his song *For Every Man There's a Woman.*" (The photo here was furnished to me by Sam Arlen, Harold Arlen's son, whom I interviewed a few days after Tony's interview. He brought up some photos from his basement archives. And there it was—like a miracle—a fifty-six year old photo of a young Harold Arlen playing the piano and an even younger Tony Martin singing during rehearsals for the film *Casbah.*)

About Tony's favorites: "My theme—*I'll See You in My Dreams*—I have always liked that song. It's my sentimental favorite. My financial favorite....(he chuckles with a tilt of his head).... is *Begin the Beguine* and, also, *There's No Tomorrow*—(a song borrowed from the Italian classic *O Sole Mio*)—they are my best money-makers." *There's No Tomorrow* is a song completely owned by Tony Martin. Another of Tony's evergreens is his 1951 recording of *I Get Ideas,* thought salacious at the time, as most pop songs then did not have sexual innuendo in them. Nevertheless, that song, taken from the 1932 Argentine Tango *Adios Muchachos,* is one of his best. And, who could forget his version of *Kiss of Fire* in 1952, another song taken from a classic, Villoldo's 1913 tango *El Choclo,* or *Stranger in Paradise* in 1954 from the Broadway hit *Kismet.* Sorry if I overlooked those earlier hits *To Each His Own* and *Tonight We Love.* Tony did especially well with many songs adapted from the classics.

At this point I handed Tony a tattered copy of *Song Hits* magazine from 1940 that I picked up a few days earlier at a collectibles show. Tony's photo was on the cover and some of the songs he was associated with were featured inside.

"Where the heck did you get that?" Tony mused, "That goes back a ways—but, you know, I remember it like it was yesterday." Tony Martin was the subject of many a magazine article or celebrity book during those days; his good looks targeted him for romantic stories linked to big-time movie stars including Lana Turner. But, Tony was always considered to be a "good guy," being one of Hollywood's nicest people.

86

And he is still one of the nicest people in Hollywood where he has been happily married to dancer Cyd Charisse for forty-nine years. Cyd, of course, worked with the supreme dancer Fred Astaire in two memorable 1950's films, *The Bandwagon* and *Silk Stockings,* and also starred in the timeless movie *Brigadoon,* all were terrific motion pictures and her best work ever. Tony and Cyd are so well suited to one another. Together they wrote an autobiography, *The Two Of Us,* in 1976.

A staunch member of The Society of Singers, Tony Martin was honored with a Lifetime Achievement Award celebration at Hollywood's Beverly Hilton Hotel on October 23, 1992. The "singer's" hotel, known among singers as Mary's Place, was decorated to recreate the old Cocoanut Grove nightclub glory days where Tony performed. Tony is a founding member of the Society and one of its staunchest supporters. Ella Fitzgerald presented the "Ella" trophy to him, saying, "I hope you don't catch my cold," as she kissed him. "Baby, I'd like to catch your rhythm!" Tony replied. It was a night to remember attended by many of his peers. Johnny Mathis sang *Begin the Beguine,* Joe Williams sang *Lover Come Back To Me,* Mel Tormé sang *The Tenement Symphony,* all Martin favorites, and Cyd danced: "I could have dated Frank Sinatra or even Dino, but Tony was to me another Valentino." she said. It was a great night.

Tony's performance the night after our interview at Carnegie Hall was absolutely amazing, belying his age, with a voice as hearty as when he serenaded his lovely co-stars in those romantic movies over 40 years ago. His brief vocal salutes to some of his songs during our interview the day before were apparently precursors to the events that would follow the next evening. Tony was almost overcome by the crowd's enthusiasm and affection, "This was the most thrilling moment of my life. If I had to retire, now would be the time." Tony has always performed at many clubs throughout the last 30 years.

Forget about his retirement, folks. I happen to know that my friend Tony Martin has bookings set clear into the 21st Century. Not bad for a *singer* who has four stars on the *Hollywood Walk of Fame.*

Guy Mitchell in his Mitch Miller Columbia Days.
(Guy Mitchell Collection)

GUY MITCHELL

No Longer Singing The Blues

What an exhilarating experience reminiscing about Guy Mitchell *with* Guy Mitchell at his Las Vegas home. Fresh from appearances in Nashville, Guy's enthusiasm is not unlike his peppy originals *My Truly, Truly Fair* and *The Roving Kind,* some of the delightful songs I enjoyed so much as a youngster, songs that established Guy as a singing star back in the early fifties. Those top-selling recordings were produced under the tutelage of Columbia Records master A & R (Artists and Repertoire) man, Mitch Miller. Miller had first offered the songs *The Roving Kind* and *My Heart Cries for You* to Frank Sinatra, who, although experiencing a serious career reversal at the time, turned Miller down cold: "So I called Guy Mitchell, and he recorded both sides, which became instant hits, "Miller said. Miller also coined Guy Mitchell's adopted name, lending his own full first name to Guy for his new surname. Guy's 1956 blockbuster, *Singing the Blues,* arranged by Ray Conniff, was number one for 26 weeks and became the biggest selling record between the '50s and '70s. In fact, the 1993 version of the Guinness Book of Who's Who of '50's Music is dedicated to Guy, as the man who started it all with that recording.

A few weeks ago, while visiting singer Jerry Vale, he explained that it was Guy Mitchell who introduced him to Mitch Miller in 1950: "I was singing in a club on Long Island and Jerry was the house singer. I said to my manager, 'Hey, there's a kid out there singing, and he's singing *better* than me.' So I asked Jerry to come to my dressing room and told him that he was very good—and he said, 'Thank you very much, Mr. Mitchell.' and I told him I'm not a 'Mr',—and that just *Guy* would be okay. So I took his number down and got hold of Mitch and the rest is history, as they say."

That introduction and eventual association with Mitch Miller established Jerry Vale as a singing star, too, along with the impressive stable of performers then at Columbia records, including Tony Bennett, Rosemary Clooney, Frankie Laine, and Johnny Ray. Although once a classical music (oboe) performer, Mitch Miller was an under-appreciated star-maker who was criticized by many, but produced an amazing quantity of popular records that sold extremely well and were adored by most of the public, if not the critics, thereby creating more singing stars than any other record producer of his time. All of Miller's protégés advanced to even greater success, graduating into their own solo careers. "We were all unknown quantities, Richard. Miller made us. He took a chance on us."

In his book *Lucky Old Son,* Frankie Laine noted, "We ended up enjoying a long string of successes together, and from the start Mitch demonstrated a talent for setting off voices in original, if not downright quirky, musical settings. Who else would've put a harpsichord on a Rosemary Clooney record, or backed Guy Mitchell with swooping French horns?"

"No matter when I perform, Richard, the people want to hear the old hits, like *Belle, (Belle, Belle, My Liberty Belle), Sparrow (Sparrow in the Treetop), Heart, (My Heart Cries for You), Roving (One of the Roving Kind),* and *Pittsburgh (Pittsburgh, Pennsylvania)*—you know what I mean. So I still sing them—and they give you standing ovations. And you can't do a medley—they want the whole song as you originally did it the first time. It's an osmosis between you and the audience. They even start singing with you after the first few bars. They know all the words, Richard."

Guy Mitchell honestly appreciates and respects his audience. "Rich, in your first book, the Trumpet book *(The Best Damn Trumpet Player)* you said Woody Herman would've given up if he had to play stuff he did twenty years before. I don't have that luxury."

For his work at Columbia, Guy earned a spot in the Columbia Records Hall of Fame, was honored with a star on the Hollywood Walk of Fame, and won *Billboard Magazine's* Triple Crown Award for an artist who hit the #1 spot, sold best in stores, and was most played on jukeboxes, all simultaneously. Only a few have achieved that position.

"But, listen, Richard, I also played with the Big Bands. I sang with Harry James at a special concert, and spent two weeks playing with Tommy and Jimmy Dorsey when they made up to keep the bands together." Guy also toured briefly with Stan Kenton and Lionel Hampton: "I was supposed to be the headliner, Rich, but when Hamp played his great theme *Flying Home,* I said to him afterwards, 'You *are* the headliner.'"

Formerly Albert Cernick, Guy Mitchell was born in Detroit on February 27, 1927. His Yugoslavian born parents moved from Colorado and then to LA in 1938. As a kid, Guy auditioned for the movies while singing on radio station KFWB in Hollywood, but the family moved on to San Francisco and Guy settled down to life as an apprentice saddle-maker and part-time rancher.

"My singing career started at three, they tell me, at Yugoslav weddings. In high school I would ride in rodeos, but, when I didn't win any money riding bulls and bucking horses, I would sing for some bucks in

"Richard–Why I went broke in the cattle business. Guess you have to feed 'em." A little joke sent to me by today's Guy Mitchell.
(Betty & Guy Mitchell Collection)

the barn. I only did that to make my way home so I could get back to school by Monday morning.

"I really didn't want to be a singer, but I could sing well and I really dug Al Jolson, Perry Como, Sinatra and Crosby. But, if I had to decide, one or the other, it'd be horses and rodeos and ranchin'. In the Navy, I ended up singing with the Navy band. Ray Anthony had a band on another ship next to us—and I wound up singing with his Navy band. When I got out, I went back to the saddle shop and rodeoing. But, I also liked music, so I auditioned for western singer Dude Martin's radio show—you know—country—pop stuff. They kept asking me to sing more songs and I went on the air. It didn't hit me though until I was on the air—and guys at the rodeo heard me and said I sounded terrific——and the advice that I'd get to buy a ranch a lot quicker by singing for good money than rodeoing. Then, I heard (pianist-bandleader) Carmen Cavallaro's singer got sick at the Mark Hopkins (a famous hotel in San Francisco) and they needed a singer right away." Guy figured that ranch he desired would be attained sooner singing with a name band like Cavallaro, so he hustled up to MCA (Music Corporation of America, who managed many performers), and volunteered to sing even without the presence of a piano.

"I said, I don't need a piano. What do you want to hear?" Guy sang *Pretending,* Nat Cole's then popular recording." They liked it. So we went over to the Mark Hopkins and there was a line of guys on each side waiting to audition. I really couldn't wait on this line—I wasn't being pig-headed, mind ya,—I had to get back to the rodeo, so I said to myself—'this settles it, I'm going back to the rodeo.' But this MCA guy let me up first with Cavallaro, and I sang Frankie Laine's hit, *Mam'selle,* and got the job. I couldn't believe it! Guy made his first recording with Carmen Cavallaro on Decca.

"In those days," Guy went on, "I liked Perry Como so much that, while practicing my singing I subconsciously began sounding like him, and Perry, who was living out on Long Island (King's Point)—all he would play was Bing Crosby records. The best advice we singers received from producers and A & R men was 'sing like yourself'.'"

Movie wise, Guy's first film at Paramount, *Those Redheads from Seattle,* with Rhonda Fleming, Gene Barry, and Teresa Brewer, was followed by *Red Garters* with Rosemary Clooney, his former singing counterpart at Columbia. Guy co-starred with Audie Murphy, the World War II hero turned actor in *Whispering Smith,* a television series during the '60s, followed by appearances on shows starring Ed Sullivan, Arthur Godfrey, Milton Berle, Dinah Shore, Mike Douglas, and on almost every other popular variety show. Guy would actually host some of those shows and as a result he was offered his own show, *The Guy Mitchell Show* on ABC in 1957-'58.

Recalling an unusual adventure during Guy's first appearance at the Copacabana Nightclub in New York evoked some humorous memories: "I turned down doing the Copa a couple of times, but I finally agreed to do it—because you have to do the Copa just once—even though to me it was a snake-pit—really was. But I went and did it anyway. The first night, Richard, became a hit because—right in the middle of all these pop songs—like *Roving* and *Truly Fair,* and maybe some standards like *Body and Soul*...and maybe an Italian song...*I Have But One Heart,* but right in the middle I threw in a country medley—and would you believe—at the sophisticated—supposedly—Copa—they went nuts! I even had to sing it upstairs (in the lounge) for the staff. Isn't that somethin' else?"

"What songs were they?" I asked.

"One of them was a Merle Haggard song....(he sings) *I know that you have been fooling around with me right from the start—but I'll take back my ring while I take back my heart.* And one of the numbers was the *Wabash Cannon Ball.* Can you believe it? And when I did my Wallace Beery ('40s Hollywood actor with a gravelly voice) impression, Red Buttons, who was the comic, fell off the stool, saying, 'That's not Wallace Beery—that's Jules Podell' (infamous manager of the Copa). It brought down the house. Things like that made opening night a hit. Isn't that wild?"

As Kathryn Crosby revealed to me that Bing always did, Guy Mitchell also sings all day long: "Throughout the day I sing all kinds of music, Richard. I'm a singer, and so I always sing."

Guy's advice to up-and-comers: "Take all the {music} lessons you can. The musicians do, and your voice is an instrument, too. Find a very good teacher, because anyone can hang out a shingle. You can tell a good teacher by their product." Guy's teacher was Gene Byram, who also taught Frankie Laine (when he lost his voice), Judy Garland, and the HiLo's singing group.

"The reason for the lessons, Richard, is—no matter how good a voice you have—when you sing three shows a night and close, then open the next day somewhere else, you're going to have your first case of laryngitis. A good teacher helps you avoid that problem. No voice— no jobs."

Guy Mitchell retired from the singing business for health and personal reasons throughout the '60s and '70s. He returned to raising cattle and quarter horses on a ranch in Idaho. In-between Guy suffered from a rare condition known as leucoplakia (of the throat), and was cured, he says, by the power of prayer. "It's funny, the fringe benefit of the illness was I sing like I did in my twenties—like *Truly Fair*—I sing those songs in the same key as I did then. That's got to be a miracle." Guy said.

By the late '70s Guy ventured back. "I went broke in the cattle business. I was away from show business for almost 15 years. They came looking for me at the ranch. They were doing a tribute to Arthur Godfrey and Mitch Miller, with all the old crew, and this guy (John Quincy Adams with PBS in New York), believe it or not, came all the way from New York City to find me—and I don't even know how he found this little town—they have a population of 1200—and they talked me into going to New York for this tribute. I was too scared to come back." But, he did. And he goes on and on singing all over the world. His 1980's release of *Always on My Mind* and *Wind Beneath My Wings* continue to sell today along with his re-issues of his early recordings.

Guy admires his fellow singers: "It's a photo finish between Jolson, Sinatra and Damone for the guys, but I really enjoy listening to all the singers. I especially enjoy Como and Crosby's early stuff, and I enjoy Ray Charles too."

Married to Betty, "For more years than she can remember," Guy chuckles as he glances at a smiling Betty in the kitchen where she is preparing a saucy, garlicky dish, "We both turned 70, Rich." The Mitchells, who have two children, and five grandkids, simply look great.

Recently, a double CD with some fifty songs has been issued in Australia where Guy is a hands down favorite. It's called *The Ultimate*

Guy Mitchell Collection and contains a Christmas song he wrote called *Dusty, The Magic Elf.*

My lifelong affection for Guy Mitchell and his music was a thirst never quenched until today when the years were bridged and punctuated on a common ground, gregarious get-together that was a total pleasure for me, a fan and a writer. Guy is in the midst of writing his autobiography, so get one when it comes out and learn even more. I had a lot to thank Guy Mitchell for, and I did!

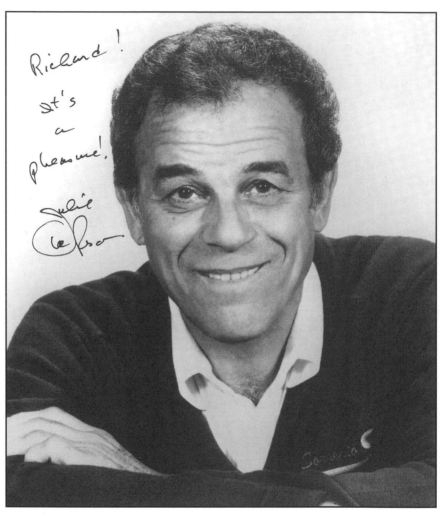

Music Man Julius La Rosa sent this great photo just for the book.
(Julius La Rosa Collection)

JULIUS La ROSA

The Radio Man's Son Sings for His Supper.

When Julius La Rosa and I got together during the summer of 1997, we discovered we lived only a few blocks from one another during the mid 1940's in Brooklyn, New York. You could find me glued to my Admiral playing mostly Bing while Julie was dreaming of singing like Frank Sinatra.

"In Grover Cleveland High School I was the vocalist with the school dance band. We sang mostly dance charts. Then I heard Sinatra. Before him a singer was just an adjunct to a band—always singing in tempo, never paying much attention to the lyrics. He taught me that songs are really little poems. He was the first to put a comma here, a hyphen there, three dots here, and a period there. What he was doing was telling the story as he interpreted it. Before that, a singer sang (Julie sings) *I love you truly*—but Frank sang (Julie sings again) *I love you-tru-ly,* giving the words meaning—interpreting the song the way the composer intended. Ask any singer my age and they will tell you that Sinatra was their major influence."

Julie, as he likes to be called, joined the Navy after high school and wound up in Pensacola, Florida, aboard a ship, an electronics technician. Arthur Godfrey (a great CBS radio personality once known as the Warbling Banjoist and emcee of *Arthur Godfrey Time,* a very popular radio show which later graduated to TV as *The Arthur Godfrey Show*) was there earning his Navy "Wings" which meant he had to qualify by landing and taking off from an aircraft carrier six times. "Someone—to this day I don't know who it was—a kid in my division—got word to him to catch their shipmate at the enlisted men's club. He did, and heard me sing *The Song Is You* and *Don't Take Your Love from Me.* and after the show he said to me, 'When you get out of the Navy—look me up— I've got a job for you.'"

Julie followed through on exactly November 19, 1951, and began singing on Godfrey's radio show. "I had no show-business experience. The six months I spent on the radio show gave me a chance to get comfortable before I was to join his television program. And, God bless (bandleader) Archie Bleyer. He was a major influence early-on. He saw I was just a kid, so he took me under his wing."

Archie Bleyer made a professional singer out of an inexperienced Julius La Rosa. A conservative gentleman, Bleyer was actually an excellent leader of men. A foremost writer of stock arrangements before the Big Band Era, Bleyer arranged and conducted an orchestra at Earl Carroll's Club in Hollywood during the 1930's, according to music historian George Simon.

"My first hit was unexpected. The song *Anywhere I Wander* had been recorded by Tony Bennett, Mel Tormé—and others—remember—in those days everyone would record the same song—but nobody had a hit with it. I liked the song (it came from the film *Hans Christian Andersen*) and sang it on the Godfrey radio and Wednesday night television shows a number of times. We got a lot of mail asking 'where can I buy the record?' I wasn't recording at the time. That was when Archie decided to start Cadence Records."

"The first Cadence record was *Anywhere I Wander?*" I guessed easily. It became a big hit for Julie.

"Yes,"Julie said, "and the record catalog number was 1230—a number I'll never forget for two reasons—1-2-30 is both my birthday and the catalog number of my first recording."

Another big hit for Julie at the time was the serendipitous and charming *Eh, Cumpari,* a Sicilian folk song similar in structure to *Old McDonald Had a Farm* with instruments instead of animals. "*Eh, Cumpari* means—well—you get married and you ask a friend to be best man—you are *cumpari*. It's a very close relationship between two people. A friend has a child—you are asked to be Godfather—we are now *cumpari*", Julie explained, "I had a lot of fun recording that song. Everyone loves it. It's infectious like Rosemary Clooney's *Come-on-a-My House*. It is a Sicilian song I sang as a kid."

Proud of his Italian roots, Julius La Rosa nevertheless told me a very amusing story about his trip to Italy: "I was visiting my uncle in Palermo, Sicily, and asked to see where my father was born. He took me to an area of the city comparable to what we call Hell's Kitchen, on the West side of Manhattan. When I got back to the hotel I sent him a telegram: 'Dad, saw where you were born. Glad you moved.' "Julie's dad was the quintessential radio repair man. He opened and closed a number of shops during his life—eternally searching for that better, more lucrative location. "He was known as Charlie, the Radio Man," Julie said.

Julie recounted the most infamous event of his life, his on-the-air firing by his somewhat tyrannical boss, Arthur Godfrey. "Well, I broke a rule. I hired a manager. You couldn't have a manager when you worked on the Godfrey show. Godfrey called William Paley, CBS Chairman, and told him my new manager, Tommy Rockwell of General Artists, informed him that in the future all dealings with Julius La Rosa had to go through his office. I've been told Paley said to him, 'You hired him on the air—so fire him on the air', and Godfrey did while millions were watching." It was October 4, 1953.

After singing his song *Manhattan,* Godfrey summarily executed him: "That was Julie's swan song with us. He goes out on his own now, as his own star, to be seen on his own show. Wish him Godspeed, as I do." Godfrey declared.

"Did you say anything to Godfrey afterwards?"

"Yes. After the show I thanked him for giving me my break. It was all cordial, no rancor. In an interview many years later, Godfrey said: 'The only SOB that ever said *thank you* was that kid, La Rosa.'"

Young and handsome Julie La Rosa started performing in clubs and theaters all over the country. "I worked where they still had live shows and had to learn my job in front of the public—how to control an audience, what tools to use, what taste was." He later toured and recorded for a while with my friend Larry O'Brien and the world-famous Glenn Miller Orchestra. "I've played them all, including Vegas. But it took a long time to learn stage presence," Julie said, "On radio and TV it's relatively easy. On a live stage, it's something else. Once, in 1955, I shared a bill with Ella Fitzgerald—in fact—she was the *extra added attraction* on the show—can you imagine that? Anyway, we started talking between shows. I told her I had a lot to learn and she told me it took her 10 years before she got comfortable on stage. I can honestly say that it took me 15 years. If you are not doing it right—they (the audience) start to talk, and you can lose them."

Some tried to make a rock-type teen idol of Julius La Rosa via a 1958 movie entitled *Let's Rock* with Paul Anka and Danny & The Juniors. It didn't work. "I will someday find and buy every print of that movie and burn them," he laughed. It was the only movie Julie ever made.

In 1969, Julie took a job on New York's then great radio station WNEW, where my friend William B. Williams held court mornings with the legendary *Make Believe Ballroom* for so many years. Like Willie, Julie talked, played records, and hosted guests weekdays from one to four until 1977, when the station changed hands, and he wasn't in the plans of the new owners.

"It's a whole different thing when you have to sit in front of a mike for four hours at a clip. The entire show was done *ad lib*—totally spontaneous. I enjoyed every minute. I learned while I worked and people listened. I always apologized for on the air mistakes and the listeners appreciated that. I loved working alongside William B. Williams, Ted Brown, and my friend, newscaster and music interviewer Mike Prelee." Earlier this year Julie was a guest on Mike's radio show *In The Spotlight* on New Jersey's WVNJ.

One of Julius La Rosa's best albums is the recent Candlewood Records offering of *Better Than Ever.* Besides being a very good representation of Julie's singing, the musicians are well-chosen. Tenor-alto Ted Nash, bass player David Finck, guitarists Gene Bertoncini and Bucky Pizzarelli, and conductor/arranger Bill Waranoff are the personnel responsible for this terrific album. Julie is very animated in the songs *Just in Time* and *Something's Gotta Give* (on which he really swings). But, I prefer the serious side of Julius La Rosa. When you listen to him sing *Here's That Rainy Day,* you will understand why he has such a legion of fans following him for so many years. I also like the way he vocalizes an old favorite, *My Foolish Heart.*

A few weeks ago while I was appearing with veteran disk jockey, Jack Ellsworth, when promoting my last book, *Song Stars,* on radio station WLIM, Jack offered 10 copies of the book to the first 10 callers who could correctly identify a certain singer. The song was *Once to Every Heart.* To our surprise the entire telephone board lit up within 10 seconds, every one of the callers correctly identifying the culprit as Julius La Rosa. "Look at that," said a surprised Jack Ellsworth, "it's fantastic—they *know* who it is." When I told Julie, he was also surprised:

"My fans are civilized and loyal," he said, "Thank God for those wonderful people. They allow a lot of us (singers) a way to make a living. I'm grateful to every one of them."

Julie lives up along the Hudson River, close to Manhattan, with his wife Rory, in a split-level house. "If I didn't marry that lady, I'd be on a funny-farm today." Julie said, "We have two great kids. Chris is an acoustic engineer who was born on the fourth of July. Till he was five he thought the fireworks were all for him.

"Maria—actually—Maria Lucia Teresa La Rosa Smith—just graced our family with a first grandchild, Robert Terence Smith, Jr. Now we are really a complete family."

Julie and I are old Brooklyn Dodger fans. After they left Julie swung over to the New York Mets and I migrated (not physically) to the Bronx to cheer for the New York Yankees.

Julie told me an interesting career story. When he first joined Godfrey, a reviewer called him "callow." Cast members told him to ignore it. "I did. Who knew what *callow* meant. That night I looked it up. The reviewer was right. I was immature and inexperienced." Several days later legendary songwriter Sammy Cahn, who wrote *It's Magic, Jealous Lover, I Fall in Love Too Easily, High Hopes, The Tender Trap, Time After Time, Day by Day,* and many others, came in to the studio: "...and he wants to meet *me. The* Sammy Cahn! He thanks me for singing his songs. Can you imagine that? However, to this day I'm convinced Sammy came to offer encouragement rather than to express thanks. I didn't know it then, of course, but it fits the man who wrote, 'Too late we find, a word that's warm and kind, is more than just a passing token.....' Look to *his* heart!

"All this may sound naive, but it's what I believe. I loved Sammy Cahn."

Sammy Cahn is wonderful, all right, but it takes a voice like Julius La Rosa's to effectively place songs like that directly into your heart.

**Joe & Jillean Williams just sent me this photo of Joe.
Check out the wrist watch (Joe Williams Collection)**

JOE WILLIAMS

Every Day He Happily Sings the Blues

Catching up to venerable blues vocalist Joe Williams is not an easy routine even in the 1990's. Fresh from a couple of gigs at New York's famed Blue Note jazz club with the Count Basie Orchestra, directed by Grover Mitchell, where he put on an absolutely remarkable show of both old and new favorites to standing ovations, Joe, now resting at home between tours, became victim to my jingling of his memory bank divulging the history of his bounteous career. I allowed him no rest as he slumped deeply into an easy chair, unlike the over six foot frame we are used to seeing when he's standing loosely on stage with those large eyes and flashing teeth.

Born seventy-nine years ago in Cordele, Georgia, Joe was blessed with a dedicated mother who, under difficult conditions, took him to Chicago and kept him in school. "Life was very hard and I worked at any job I could find," he recalled thoughtfully, "I was a man-child in the streets. I worked at selling newspapers, carrying ice, anything—and I finished three years of high school, which was difficult in those days." His mother interested him in music, although he wanted to be a baseball player, but, he said, "I drifted into playing the piano and listening to the strongly dramatic—very rhythmic urban blues." His other teacher was the radio. He listened carefully to Duke Ellington broadcasting from the Cotton Club. He was also impressed by the powerful Paul Robeson and Lawrence Tibbett, the great operatic voices of the 1930's.

His absolute influence? "That'll be Joe Turner," Joe replies, "I never sang the blues before until I heard Turner and decided that's how it's supposed to be. That, for me, was the difference. Turner was a great body standing like a statue out there and just belting out one after another."

Joe Turner was the great robust blues singer who earlier played the Kansas City circuit accompanied by Pete Johnson's piano. He would sometimes sing all night. In 1941, Turner was signed by Duke Ellington who found him fascinating. "He turns every song into a great blues song," Ellington said. Joe also credits Ethel Waters and Herb Jeffries as strong musical influences. "Like Joe Turner, they sang with great feeling," he said, and also mentioned the names of Perry Como with Ted Weems and Pha Terrell with Andy Kirk.

Joe Williams' (formerly Joseph Goreed) big band credentials began at age 16 with Johnny Long's band. (That's when his mother and aunt chose the name *Williams* as Joe would go around and ask local bandleaders on the south side of Chicago to let him sing with their band). Next was work with Erskine Tate and Jimmie Noone's (in Chicago,) sometimes performing with all three at the same time. Then he performed with Coleman Hawkins, Lionel Hampton (where he was paid eleven dollars a night to start) and finally toured with Andy Kirk's big band in 1946. "I was with Hampton four months or so, but I never recorded with him because of the recording ban. That's when I first met Frank Sinatra. He was with Dorsey at the Paramount. Dorsey backed his singers better than any band. I learned from that meeting." Joe's legendary tenure with Count William Basie existed from 1954 to early 1961. It's where Joe established his name, expanded his repertoire, and, it is acknowledged, helped increase the fame of the Basie band as well. That great locomotive band was the perfect showcase for his range and versatility. When people think about Joe Williams, it's almost always about that association with Basie. Joe's definitive recording *Everyday I Have the Blues* was the superior one recorded with Basie in 1955. It became his theme song. On that same album Joe included *Going to Chicago* and *Alright, Okay, You Win,* two of his long-standing classics.

After Basie, Joe performed in front of Harry "Sweets" Edison's quintet for a while and has freelanced ever since. He has collaborated with jazz pianist George Shearing on an album and completed two with trumpeter Thad Jones and jazz drummer Mel Lewis. Joe has returned to Basie time and again, even with then ghost—bandleader Frank Foster in 1992. In 1984 Joe appeared in Boston at Symphony Hall with Sarah Vaughan, backed by the masterful pianist Norman Simmons and a blue-ribbon trio.

"You have performed with just about every great jazz singer and even some non-jazz singers," I noted.

"Oh, Yeah! Ella—Ella—and Lena, and Dinah, and Sarah—Dizzy (Gillespie), Carmen (McRae), everybody, and that means Marlena Shaw, Diane Schuur, Diane Reeves, and Cleo Laine, too."

Over the years Joe Williams has shown himself to be at home with all forms of rhythms: blues ballads; romantic standards; bright, up-tempo things, and soulful blues. The range is part of the Williams mystique. With a pillowy voice and regal presence, he exudes confidence, being now the elder statesman of blues singing.

"In 1994—after wanting to do an album of spirituals for some time, I recorded the album *Feel The Spirit*—you know, stuff like *Go Down Moses* and *The Lord's Prayer.* I had to do that, Richard. And I'm glad I did.

"They come to hear me—today. 'What's he doin' now?' they wonder. So they give me their gift—and time is their most valuable gift. When you walk out to standing ovations you know that something is happening. The people come once again, and for years."

Joe and I talked more about our friend Count Basie. My wife, Jean, and I interviewed Bill and Catherine Basie back in 1982. Jean and Catherine got to know one another while Bill, his valet, and I helped him change from street clothes to concert cloth. Bill, after suffering a heart attack in 1976 and a victim of severe arthritis, needed help at this point in his life, even simply dressing himself.

We agreed that Bill Basie was a gentle, very nice man. "His band members loved him too," Joe said, "He gets out of the way and let's them play. He lets the guys play so they have pride in what they do because they are doing it, "Joe went on, "How do you conduct feelings? That's the reason they have sounded so good for all that time. If there were problems within the band, we would always straighten it out without involving Basie. We were artists that tried to act like artists. The musicians were all proud men who believed in getting the music right."

When Count Basie celebrated his 80th birthday in 1983 at a Greenwich Village, New York, night club, Joe blew out the cake candles. Basie called him his Number One son. Joe Williams and Bill Basie never shook hands when they greeted one another—they vigorously hugged every time. While with Basie, Joe was voted best blues singer five times in the Downbeat Magazine reader's poll.

"He spent a lot of time kidding me," Joe said, "but in that kidding there was always a lesson."

We talked about what Tony Bennett once revealed to me. Asking Tony if a performer is the same person on stage as he is off stage, Tony said he became distinctly someone different: "When I come out to sing, I change and emotionalize and begin to feel the audience out there, and my songs come across more personalized-more sensitive—more dramatic—and I love it." he said.

Joe agreed: "Of course that's the way it is, alright. First of all you're relating to everything pertaining to what you are doing. Everything else is shut out. It has to be. In over forty years of performing that's the way I do it. I choose my own songs and do them exactly the way I feel them at the time."

Joe Williams hangs out with musicians, mostly old-time collaborators. John Levy is a bass player whom he has known and worked with since the '40s. John is now 85. Their friendship is still strong. It's the same with Norman Simmons, whose trio has solidly backed Joe on many live and recorded performances.

"Joe," I pointed out, "you are considered the last of the jazz/blues singers of the Big Band Era. How do you think history will record your place in jazz singing?"

"I have no idea. I am a singer, and I sing. I sing only songs that I feel I can do well. Be it Billy Joel's stuff (he recorded *Just the Way You Are*) or Cole Porter. I don't sing today for that reason. (being memorialized). Maybe I have to think more about that question." He smiles and hunches his shoulders from the easy chair.

Joe had some advice for up and coming singers: "They have to find their own way. They have to put in the time, the hardships, the experiences. They have to approach something new-something different. You can't imitate the great distinctive voices. When a group of singers tries to sound alike because of a current popular sound, it doesn't work. I remember when everyone was chasing Bing Crosby. There was (Russ) Columbo, Perry Como, Dean Martin, Pat Boone, and so many others. They found their own way eventually. It got them started. But they had to find their own way in the end." Joe never copied his predecessor

106

Jimmy Rushing, although he often sang with him, because the distinctive sound of Rushing was so unique. "I wouldn't have attempted to approach what he was doing. Like Louis Armstrong and Billie (Holiday)—that distinctive sound is what you don't get involved in at all," he said. "It's true that the old songs were best. As Norman Simmons wisely says, 'when singers perform today nobody falls in love.' It's different now."

Joe Williams album *Nothing But The Blues* for which he won the Grammy in 1985 found him in prime form performing with jazzmasters Eddie Vinson, tenor Red Holloway, organist Brother Jack McDuff, Ray Brown, and other All Stars. Other albums have included a who's who of players—too many to mention here.

"You seem to get better with each successive album," I said, "They say you have created a more interesting singer in yourself in your later years."

"I hope so because you should get better as you go."

The summer of 1991 found Joe Williams being honored by the Society of Singers in Las Vegas. Henry Mancini, Greg Morris, Keely Smith, Della Reese, Robert Goulet, Billy Eckstine, Nancy Wilson, Al Hibbler, and Marsha Warfield were there among many others saluting his lifetime of success as a great singer of the blues. His lovely wife of 40 years, Jillean, was among the faithful. A remarkable pleasant person, Jillean is English, raised in Surrey, a great fan of Winston Churchill, and faithful to the Queen. Although Joe and Jillean live in Las Vegas, Joe never sings there. "I wouldn't work any of the main rooms there unless they dealt me the full treatment," he said.

It was in July of 1996 at the Dakota Bar in St. Paul when Joe launched into the great favorites *Dimples, CC Rider, I Got It Bad and That Ain't Good, Tenderly,* and *Satin Doll.* "I don't remember feeling that good. I think every pore in my body was open that night, Richard. I am 78 years old now but I feel like forty. It was one of my best." They say the audience was swaying and hooting uproariously, enjoying every moment. He sings so clearly with such fine diction.

A serious golfer, Joe has golfed around the world just as he has sung around the world. He's been blessing our living rooms since the early fifties and he keeps going, whether he is playing Bill Cosby's father-in-law in a comedy with a presence as big as his voice or appear-

Joe Williams still sings for his supper.
(Richard Grudens Collection)

ing on a musical program. He readily hops on planes, racing from city to city dishing up those great songs of his.

If you are lucky enough to get to see him it will be as though you have discovered a new singer, not the elder statesman of blues. He's great to watch. As a singer he's a great actor.

The name of Joe Williams will always be synonymous with great blues singing, impeccable and excellent. I am fortunate to count him among my friends.

JERRY VALE

He Still Hears the Applause

I had always wanted to interview Jerry Vale. Like Perry Como, who is *his* hero, Jerry is one of those calm, pleasant and romantic singers who consistently command a legion of admirers. After many years of scuttled opportunities, Jerry and I finally got together recently on a beautiful fall Sunday evening backstage at Westbury Music Fair on Long Island, where he was appearing for a one-night stand co-starring with comedian Dom De Luise. While waiting for Jerry to arrive, I ran into old friend Dom and chatted for a while about his friend, Music Man Dean Martin, and about Dom's frequent appearances on Dean's television show.

Jerry Vale's presentation to Joe DiMaggio of Jerry's gold record of National Anthem played at Major League games. (For Baseball Hall of Fame) (Jerry Vale Collection)

Jerry Vale sent me this early photo. He was always a silver fox.
(Richard Grudens Collection)

When Jerry arrived, photographer Bill De Betta and I ushered him quickly into his dressing room, sat him down on the couch while still in his windbreaker sporting his famous silver shocks of hair, and taped that long awaited interview. Jerry arrived at 6:15 PM and had to be on stage at 7:00. We squeezed 30 minutes from that tight schedule, took some photos, and helped him get ready for his appearance. Although still in pain with a knee that recently underwent arthroscopic surgery, he sprinted carefully down the ramp to center stage at exactly seven, as he was introduced with a fanfare and medley of his standards. I watched him for a while from the wings, his white shocks of hair highlighting his persona. A gratified audience was enthralled. Jerry was very uncomfortable, but you couldn't tell, "You have to go on no matter what," he said moments earlier. "all seasoned troopers know that. My knee hurts like mad, but I performed last night and I will do it again tonight."

Genero Louis Vitaliano was born 65 years ago in the Bronx where his beloved Yankees played baseball (He and manager Joe Torre are good friends, as were Mickey Mantle, Yogi Berra, Bobby Murcer, and manager Casey Stengel.)He worked at shoe-shining on the sidewalks of the Bronx at age twelve. Evander Childs High School days found him laboring in a fluorescent light factory after school, while frequently entering singing contests until he won one that earned him a spot at the local Club Del Rio. "I always wanted to become a singer after listening to Perry Como and Frank Sinatra, singing along with their records," he said, "Then, a friend of mine was going up to the club to see a friend and he asked me to take the ride with him. When we walked in they were having a singing contest—the announcer said, 'Anybody else want to sing?'...and with that my friend literally pushed me out on stage and said, 'Here he is—Jerry Como.' I sang *Far Away Places* and won the contest, so the guy offered me a job." Jerry remained performing at the Club Del Rio for over a year, receiving ten dollars a night.

"How did you know you wanted to become a professional singer?" I asked, sitting alongside him on that comfortable couch.

"When I heard the applause," he replied with that signature grin.

Jerry went on to perform at the Stardust Ballroom in the Bronx with a fourteen piece band. He began singing mostly love songs and still sings love songs today: "I like to sing songs that tell a story, have a pret-

111

ty melody, nice lyrics, and are sentimental. It was always my choice to perform that kind of material."

When singer Guy Mitchell, who was among the stable of singing stars under the direction of Mitch Miller, artists and repertoire man at CBS/Columbia,who also guided the singing careers of Rosemary Clooney, Tony Bennett, Johnny Ray, Patti Page, Frankie Laine, and others, introduced Jerry Vale to Miller, he also became one of that illustrious, industrious, prolific group who flooded the era with a great batch of great, memorable records. Jerry's first recorded hit, *Two Purple Shadows,* was followed by *Pretend You Don't See Her* (with Percy Faith's Orchestra) and *You Don't Know Me,* still three of his favorites with audiences so many years later.

Those growing times found him perfecting his craft at choice venues all over the U.S.: The Copacabana in New York, Diplomat Hotel in Hollywood, Frontier Hotel in Las Vegas, and Century Plaza in L.A. Jerry has been acclaimed in Melbourne, Australia; The Philippines; Italy, and South Africa. He was a frequent television guest on so many shows from *The Tonight Show* to *The Dean Martin Show* and had his own program entitled *Jerry Vale's World,* shot in Las Vegas back in the seventies.

Identified with numbers like *Non Dimenticar, Arriverderci Roma, Come Back to Sorrento,* and *Anema E Core,* Jerry says, "My music is like a romantic trip to Italy. They are such rich gems. I am the one who always chooses those songs to record."

**Jerry Vale and me backstage at Westbury Music Fair in August 1997.
(Photo by William Debetta)**

In early September I had visited Jack Ellsworth at radio station WLIM on Long Island while he was on the air with his daily show *Memories in Melody*. We were talking Jerry Vale and other singers. Jack's most requested Jerry Vale numbers over a long period of time are *Till the End of Time* and *Pretend You Don't See Her*. "Wow," Jerry said, "I would have thought *Ciao Ciao Bambina* or *I Have But One Heart*...or even *Because You're Mine* would have been the choices. They are my most requested. I guess it's different choices in different places."

I was telling Jerry how it was that Bing Crosby always sang around the house, according to what Kathryn revealed to me, "in the garden, or even in the shower, singing commercials or even the latest rock tunes," she said ever so proudly.

"Interesting, but I never do that," Jerry said, "I sing only during rehearsals or at engagements...never at home or when I'm alone." These days he enjoys doing benefits and sometimes working in tandem with fellow singers besides his regular schedule of performances. Recently, in Tampa, Florida, Frankie Laine told me he sang at a concert with Jerry, Don Cornell, Anna Maria Alberghetti, and Julie La Rosa. "That was for the Fiesta Italiano," Jerry clarified, "with all Italian-American performers."

Jerry has been married to former dancer and actress Rita Grable for thirty-eight years. They have a son, Robert, who is 33, and a daughter, Pamela, who is 30: "My son has a music firm, my daughter is an artist. She creates large wall murals and decorative art."

In May of 1996, Jerry was honored by a special "Ellis Island Award" bestowed on him by the National Ethnic Coalition of Italian Americans of the United States of America. "It's an organization that picks people from different backgrounds, for instance, anybody whose family came through Ellis Island into this country, whether it's your mother or father or grandfather, and they pick people who are success- ful in their chosen fields—people who have done something for society or humanity—and my wife and I worked for the Heart Fund for a long time to raise money—also for the Cancer Fund—we did work for a lot of different charities. So they asked me if I would accept this award as an outstanding citizen for the Italian-Americans. I was very pleased and proud to get it.

"You know Arthur Tracy was there and he said, 'How come nobody asked me to sing?' he said indignantly, puzzled. (Arthur Tracy was ninety-eight years old. He is the famous "Street Singer" of the twenties and thirties. He passed away on October 5th, just after our interview).

Jerry's favorite of his own work is *Mala Femmina*. "I sing better on that than I have ever sang in my life. I like the song and I seem to do it well." Perry Como's recording of *Song of Songs* is one of his favorites of the competition. Jerry is very vocal about all the other singers, always praising them. "Barbra Streisand's recording of *Why Did I Choose You* is my favorite female recording. It's a beautiful song that not many are familiar with. One of her best records, I believe."

I called off some names to get Jerry Vale's take on other singers: Frank Sinatra: "The best! What else can you say about Sinatra? There is only one Sinatra—and he's a good friend of mine."

Frankie Laine: "Frank is a great artist who gave something new to the business when he made it. I mean, he sang a song like nobody ever did."

Perry Como: "Well, you know—Como—beautiful voice—beautiful man—nobody ever came close to him as far as his outlook on life and the way he treats his family and his friends. He's just a beautiful guy, you know."

Nat Cole: "I knew Nat Cole. I had gotten to know him fairly well when I was working in Las Vegas. I also met him up in Canada while I was on tour. He was such a nice man and a very great talent."

Julius La Rosa: "I love Julius La Rosa. He's been a dear friend for many, many years, and he is one of the best singer's around. He's got the best feel of any singer. I mean, he can sing anything. He does jazz and he does it well."

William B. Williams (of WNEW, New York radio fame): "He was the best and one of the first guys to play a Jerry Vale record. I always loved the Make Believe Ballroom show that he did."

Mel Tormé: "Mel is one of the greatest artists of all time. Here's a man who can write arrangements, conduct an orchestra, compose songs, play the drums like nobody—and sing beautifully as well. Who else do you know who can do all that?"

Dick Haymes: "I love Dick Haymes, too. Nobody sang low notes like Dick Haymes. He had a good quality in his voice and when he hit those low notes it was a pleasure to listen to. A deep baritone, but he could also sing those high notes. He had quite a bit of success. He made movies with Betty Grable—with Vivian Blaine—and Jeanne Crain—he did a lot of good things. He had a problem because he was born out of this country (in Argentina). They were talking about deporting him at one time. Aside from all of that—all those people you mention—all those guys—Como, Sinatra, Dick Haymes, Frankie Laine—were all great. I look at it this way. I don't pick any one of them as my favorite—because I think they are all terrific."

That's just what Buddy Rich once said to me when I asked him to name an all-star band. "They're all giants. So how can you insult all the other giants by picking just some of them. So all of them are my favorites."

Jerry Vale's advice to up-and-coming singers is: "Just keep singing. If they keep doing it, someday—if the talent is really there—somebody will find them. Unfortunately the way the world is today, if you're not a rock artist it's hard to get records played unless you're a nostalgia artist. If I was starting today, maybe I would not be as successful. Rock and roll has taken over the airwaves. Sure, Sinatra, Como, Laine and myself are played, but it's because we have established the territory and are well-known and accepted by those who know us over the years."

Jerry admits that if he had the chance to do it over again, the one thing he would change is to have studied music more thoroughly: "I started out playing the bass for a while, but I never studied music—just played by 'ear.' I'm sorry now that I didn't really study music a lot more—I would know more about theory—I would have better timing—I would feel a lot more comfortable. For my own piece of mind, not that I have any problems, I wish I had studied music more for those reasons." So he says to anybody coming up in the business—what ever they do—sing—dance—study the music. It makes the road easier to travel.

Jerry's future? "Just keep on working as long as I can, because I love what I do. I love to be in front of the audience. I love the fact that people appreciate what I've done. I want to keep singing. Maybe when I'm about seventy—maybe I'll call it a day. I don't know. Frankie Laine is in his eighties and still singing. Maybe I'll be as fortunate."

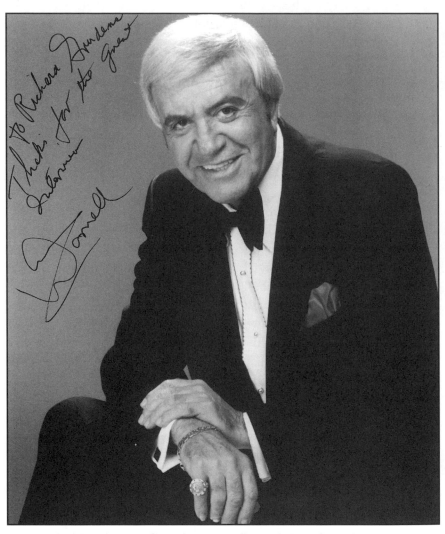

My friend, Perry Como's best golfing pal, Don Cornell–today.
(Iris Cornell Productions)

DON CORNELL

Big Voice, Big Heart

It's hard to tell who has the most enthusiasm in the Cornell family, Don or Iris. This enterprising couple has been working hard to insure a new generation, as well as the previous one, gets to hear the man with the big voice, long-respected singer Don Cornell.

He's still tall and handsome with a clear and powerful voice, "And he sings in the same key as when he was young!" a bubbly Iris said to me just today, a few days before Christmas, 1997. In concert, when Don sings *The Wind Beneath My Wings,* it's clearly dedicated to Iris, who is also his manager and inspiration, "...singing it as if only she were in the room," wrote Anthony DiFlorio III in a recent review of Don's appearance at Resorts International in Atlantic City, where he performed with full orchestra and long-time pianist and friend, Ed Cerveny. "Don meant every word of it, ending with a powerful flourish. Even though she must have heard it many times before, Iris was moved, as was the audience." he concluded.

"After losing my first wife Edith to cancer after 36 years of marriage, I was dejected and had no desire to perform. Iris changed all that for me in 1978, when we were married." Don told me, "She's been managing things successfully for 16 years now. I consider myself twice blessed.

"After first singing in local clubs in my Bronx neighborhood, I started playing guitar and singing with a band called Mickey Alpert back in the thirties at the Edison Hotel in New York City, Richard," Don recounted, "I also played and sang with The McFarland Twins (Art & George, the saxophone-playing brothers who ran a dance band in the late thirties), Al Kavelin (sharing the bandstand with vocalist Vivian Blaine), Lennie Hayton's Orchestra (jazz pianist of the late thirties previously with Paul Whiteman's King of Jazz Orchestra), and many bands in-between including Loring "Red" Nichols and His five Pennies."

Don's singing influences were decidedly Russ Columbo and Bing Crosby. "Perry Como and I agree....and many of the others too....that we looked up to Bing as the singer who started it all," declared Don at his comfortable Miami Beach home. Don's very first record date was with Bobby Hayes' Band vocalizing on a ballad called *Trust In Me,* a later hit for Eddie Fisher.

Before he was Don Cornell, Luigi Francesco Varlaro was born over on Mott Street in Lower Manhattan, "and then we moved to 181st Street, right into the Bronx's 'high society' (he chuckles). Coming from Italian immigrant parents, we had no radio or television. We entertained ourselves." Don's father, a tailor, also played the mandolin. His momma, a housewife who sang in the church choir, possessed a beautiful soprano voice. "On Sunday, my father would take out the mandolin, mother would sing, and the whole family, including my four brothers, performed for one another. It was inbred in us as in so many other Italians." Don was once an undefeated local boxer, but he gave it all up to sing.

"I acquired the name Don Cornell very simply. It was difficult to sell a name like Lou Varlaro in show business in those days, especially since Italy's dictator Mussolini had joined the Axis Countries with Hitler during the war. Every time they called out my name Lou Varlaro, there would be some boo's from the audience." Sammy said he had to change Lou's name, who looked at him with disbelief: "One night I was standing in the wings and someone called out, 'Now, here's Don Cornell,' and I'm looking around thinking, 'Who the hell is that?' And that, Richard, is how it all started." He speaks like he sings—clear and strong.

Don stepped into the big-time in 1949, with Sammy Kaye's "Swing and Sway" Orchestra. "My important recordings with Sammy were *It Isn't Fair, Daddy,* and *Harbor Lights." Serenade of the Bells* and *Stage Door Canteen* were also hits with Kaye. Here Don was able to utilize his pulsating, powerful voice to propel the band from being what they called a mild "Mickey Mouse" style band into a more respectable, versatile and assertive member of the Big Band community. "With Sammy," Don recalled, "we had an itinerary that ran from January to

January, with only one week off for Christmas." Don left Kaye to perform military service with the Army Air Corps, then later rejoined the band.

The tune *Heart of My Heart* earlier recorded with ex-Glenn Miller vocalist Johnny Desmond and singer Alan Dale is also a big request for Don at concerts: "From 1950 to 1962, I had a gold record each year. The first one was *It Isn't Fair.* That's the one mostly requested along with *I'm Yours,* (one of Don's first hits with Coral Records beginning in 1952)," Don was saying, "and we engage a full orchestra so we are able to retain the original charts when I sing these requests. The fans always expect to hear the original versions.

Don told me a little story about the original release of *It Isn't Fair,* a song he had recorded a year earlier while still with Sammy Kaye: "Unaware of the song's release, I drove up to a concert date and found lines around the block. I literally had to fight my way into the building. I discovered the recording I had made of *It Isn't Fair* was just released and was being featured on many disc jockey's shows around the country. What a surprise, and boy, what crowds filled my shows after that day."

Hold My Hand, another big Don Cornell hit (that became a # 1 hit in England, remaining on the British charts for twenty-one weeks), was featured in the 1954 movie *Susan Slept Here.* It received an Academy Award nomination, unfortunately to be eclipsed by a luckier entry *Three Coins in the Fountain.*

Don excels on so many great recordings: *That Old Feeling, Most of All, The Bible Tells Me So* (written by Roy Rogers' wife Dale Evans), *Play Some Music for Broken Hearts* (a recent # 1 title in a top 100 countdown in Ohio), *When I was a Child* (a very moving song), *Most of All,* and *Love is a Many Splendored Thing,* to mention a few. After all the hits moved on to become standards, Don's effortless classic baritone voice remained in demand for club and theater work from then right up to today. "I have always believed a song tells a story. It must be interpreted through feelings, the message must be conveyed by the singer to the listener!" Don was saying.

Lately, Don closes concerts with a tune called *Old Man Time*: "That song was given to me by my dear friend Jimmy Durante. My first job after leaving Sammy Kaye in 1950 was at Palumbo's in Philadelphia—

a very famous club—all the big names played there. I was on the bill with Durante. On about the third day he called me into his dressing room and said, 'I have a song for you. I want you to take it and put it away and don't sing it for 40 years. You're too young to understand it now.' If you look at the lyrics you can understand what he was trying to tell me."

"He gives you youth and he steals it away,
He gives you nice pretty hair and turns it gray."

"Yes. I only remember Jimmy Durante singing it, so I put it in my act. It's always a very personal experience each time I sing it,", Don told me. "And the audiences absolutely adore it," added Iris.

Don's personal performing favorite is his blockbuster hit *It Isn't Fair,* just as Tony Bennett loves to perform his evergreen *I Left My Heart In San Francisco,* and Kay Starr eternally enjoys singing the song that built her career, *Wheel of Fortune.* "You owe allegiance to those songs," Don said, quite seriously.

"Don't you ever get tired of singing it?"

"Well, I've been doing it for fifty years and it's my trademark. My new album *From Italy With Love* contains many more of the favorites I enjoy singing at concerts. Here you'll find my original Italian favorites *Mala Femmina, Ciao, Ciao Bambina, Volare,* and *Non Dimenticar.*" He also loves singing those Italian favorites at concerts.

Unlike Bing Crosby or Guy Mitchell, Don Cornell rarely sings at home, "I only sing at concerts, Richard. Singing at home is like bringing home your job. I try to take time away from singing by playing golf and otherwise relaxing. I have a big schedule set for next year, so I'm taking some time off now for a while. I will trade in my microphone for a pitching wedge."

Don's new releases *From Italy with Love, Something to Remember Me By,* and *I'll Be Seeing You* are selling very well, according to Iris. "I am amazed at the reaction to these new issues, Richard. It's like a renewal—a re-birth of Don's career. It's rewarding to see his career take off again through these CD's. People call us from all over the country to order them. Radio stations everywhere play them regularly. It's so exciting." The selections are digitally re mastered from the originals

'50s and '60s recordings and are drawn from the multi-label sources including Coral and RCA Victor. Iris sent me a copy of each album. You have to hear them to believe them. They are processed like they were just recorded today, but with the advanced technology of the '90s. "And remember Richard, some of the musicians and arrangers on these original recordings were among the finest craftsmen ever involved in music."

I asked Don for spontaneous comments on some of his peers: "Sinatra is considered the 'Chairman of the Board,' Perry Como and I have been friends for almost 60 years. He has his Rose, and I have my Iris," he says with a broad smile. "We'll be playing golf together this Tuesday. It's funny, but true—Perry and I joined the Big Bands around the same time about 60 years ago when he started with Freddie Carlone. The whole world loves Como. Tony Bennett is also a great stylist—but, although he never sang with the bands, he certainly is a dynamic performer. Mel Tormé is a brilliant composer and a great performer. Jimmy Roselli? Jimmy Roselli is the greatest Italian singer around. Guy Mitchell? I love Guy Mitchell and Jerry Vale—I know them many, many years-we worked together a number of times. Frankie Laine and I did a concert together just a few months ago. He's just dynamic and a good friend, as is Julius La Rosa. (He is referring to the very big Fiesta Italiano in Florida with Don, Julius La Rosa, Jerry Vale, accordionist Dick Contino, and Anna Maria Alberghetti). The best thing that ever happened to Julie is when he got fired by Godfrey. Dean Martin? Dean once said that everything he learned as a singer he learned from me. I'm proud of that."

If Don Cornell had to do it all over again: "I would have used my big voice more, but everybody was crooning then, so I had to go along with the wave." Don would have applied the power he performs with today, as he does with his emotionally powerful version of *I'll Walk Alone,* my personal favorite Don Cornell performance. Nobody does it better.

"Don simply walks onto center stage in his inimitable way, greets his audience, sings and, guess what? He owns the room—every inch of it," wrote author Joseph Laredo for Don's new album *Something to Remember Me By.* "We feel pangs of nostalgia when we realize that

Don Cornell is probably the last of the reigning crooners who began as "boy singers" with the Big Bands of the '40s, who is still going strong."

Somewhere along the line I recall a quote from Bing Crosby who said, when asked about up-and-coming singers at the time: "Of all the boy singers coming up, I would vote Don Cornell my favorite."

An interesting epilogue: Once, long ago, before time began, Don Cornell performed on the Major Bowes Amateur Hour and received the "gong." "I got the gong and was rudely hustled off stage. I went home in tears. But there were so many favorable phone calls that came into the studio the next day that they had me back the next week. This time I won it."

Don Cornell has been going strong ever since with Iris solidly there nestled beneath those wings we mentioned earlier. In 1963, Don was one of the first to be honored with a star on the Hollywood Walk of Fame for his contributions to the world of music, and he was inducted into The Big Band Hall of Fame in 1993. My friend, Big Band Hall of Fame President Sally Bennett was just as excited as Don and Iris. So was I.

Some singers are hard to find. Don and Iris Cornell can easily be found at 1-800-940-SING, their Miami based headquarters. You may find yourself ordering a CD or two of Don's classics.

AL MARTINO

For Music, He Has But One Heart

Al Martino, formerly Alfred Cino of Philadelphia, is a wonderful, friendly Italian ballad-style singer. Not unlike Vic Damone, Al soft-croons songs like *Here in My Heart, I Love You More and More Each Day,* and *Volare.* Al's most famous recording is his 1965 version of a million-selling tune called *Spanish Eyes,* a memorable, international favorite and undeniably a very popular composition.

In the city of Philadelphia, where he first worked as a brick-layer with his Italian immigrant dad, the young Al Martino received encouragment to seek out a singing career by an older friend, legendary vocalist and motion picture actor Mario Lanza:

"As an impressionable youngster I got started singing the same way so many others did, I listened and was influenced by other singers on the radio. There was Tony Martin, Sinatra, Perry Como—and so I bought their records and began to sing along with them. Of course, you haven't developed your own style yet—it doesn't appear until years later." I was talking to veteran vocalist Al Martino about his phenomenal career from his Beverly Hills, California home this cold and rainy New York Saturday afternoon in January. He speaks as clearly and confidently as he sings.

"I began to vocalize first with a piano, then at local clubs around Philadelphia with a trio, and then I was a winner on an *Arthur Godfrey's Talent Scouts* show, and before you know it, I was making records." Luckily, Al Martino quickly found a backer in Bill Borrelli, who had heard him on the talent contest show. "He liked the way I sang and thought I would be the perfect singer to record a song he was working on called *Here In My Heart,*" Al recalled, "So with two other financial backers, Busillo and Smith, we formed the recording company BBS Records, perhaps the very first independent record label, just to produce

123

Check out those Italian style Spanish eyes of Al Martino on this photo he sent me not too long ago. (Richard Grudens Collection)

my first recording." It was, of course, the first time that very popular song was ever sung or recorded, for, like a miracle, it went straight to number one on the charts. "We had no idea it would score that well on the charts," Al said, "even though I liked the song very much from the beginning, and it was actually written just for me." Al also states that the appearance on Godfrey's show undeniably is responsible for his early success.

Monty Kelly, an arranger and friend of Al Martino, worked diligently with him, locating and rehearsing quality studio musicians, directing the orchestra in the careful arrangement of this recording. "When you want to make a record, you simply hire an orchestra. That's the usual pattern. You don't have to have your own established orchestra to make a record," Al explained.

Al Martino brought the newly-made record to Johnny Mercer's Capitol Records: "I drove to California and took the record with the BBS label—it took me three days to get there—and tried to sell it to Capitol. I had but five days to sell it. I made a deal in Philadelphia that if I didn't sell the record to Capitol within five days, it would revert back to another manufacturer, Dave Miller, who owned a record company in Philadelphia. I had to forfeit all my royalties if Capitol didn't buy it. That was the gamble. As luck would have it, they didn't buy it. So I gave it to Mr. Miller. It became a hit, and, of course, I received no royalties."

"Nothing at all?"

"Not one penny."

"Patty Andrews and her two sisters received only fifty dollars jointly for their world-famous recording of *Bie Mir Bist Du Schoen* and had to split it three ways," I reminded Al, "and Fran Warren received but fifty dollars for her classic hit recording of *Sunday Kind of Love* made with Claude Thornhill's Orchestra—I guess it has happened to so many singers in those days." Connie Haines and Jo Stafford had reported the same thing happened to them in those days.

Another very memorable Al Martino vignette: "In the early sixties, I heard an instrumental melody on the radio called *Moon Over Naples,* which was written by German orchestra leader Bert Keampfert. It had been released in America, and I had a copy of it, but I didn't know there were lyrics written to it. Then somebody wrote a lyric, I heard it on the radio, and I didn't like the lyric at all. So I called up the publisher, and said, ' if you dump that record that's out right now, I'll give you an exclusive on a new and better lyric.' I had new lyrics written for it by songwriters Ted Snyder and Larry McCousick." That was in 1965, and it became Al Martino's biggest record. The song: *Spanish Eyes,* of course.

As this young singer's career developed, he did well singing in and for the movies. He sang the title song for the Bette Davis film *Hush...Hush Sweet Charlotte,* which led to his playing the character of Johnny Fontane in the 1972 award-winning film *The Godfather.* The tune he performed was an Italian piece entitled *O Marenariello* (*I Have But One Heart*), written by Johnny Farrow. It was perfectly suited for him. Al also successfully recorded the film's poignant theme *Speak Softly, Love.*

Al Martino has no personal favorite songs or singers to proclaim: "I consider all my songs equal to one another, *I Love You More and More Every Day, Here In My Heart, I Love You Because, Spanish Eyes,* the songs that people bought—and that became Top Ten—like *Mary in the Morning,* that's a folk song (my Al Martino favorite), and others, you know. I feel the same way about all the singers I know, too. I love and enjoy them all. I really do."

Song Star fan Gloria Sarnicola snapped this one of Al Martino on stage at Sunset Station, Las Vegas, September 1997.

Al says it's not always easy selecting a song you want to record: "The best way to hear a song is to get a good demo on it...especially from the writer. He usually will send you a lead sheet set for the piano, but that's not good enough. You have to have the writer's interpretation. The writer's interpretation is probably the best because he wrote the

126

song. Johnny Cymbal wrote the song *Mary in the Morning*—he sent me a demo of him singing it while he played the guitar. So I hired Johnny to play at the recording session." The song is one of Al's most popular recordings, one he gets requests for at concerts.

Like so many other American singers, Al Martino's records always fare better in Europe than in our own country: "People in Europe are true music lovers, "Al said, "Here in America they mostly think of just one thing—Rock and Roll, or Rap, or anything dished up and pushed upon the public by Top 40 radio. In Europe, especially the adults, they appreciate our kind of music and promote and play it consistently over the rock stuff." Al lived in England from 1953 to 1959 where he enjoyed great popularity as a performer.

Al Martino has a bevy of albums he has recorded from 1962 right up to the late eighties. Besides his Italian hits, Al did some well-produced country albums and beautifully recorded love songs, like *Strangers in the Night, Some Enchanted Evening* (the great song from Rodgers and Hammerstein's Broadway show *South Pacific*), *Make the World Go Away,* and *Somewhere My Love.*

Al doesn't vocalize much when he is at home, except when rehearsing, which he does while playing his piano. "That's the only way I can keep my voice in shape all the time...it keeps me going. "Al maintains that he sings much better today than he did yesterday, "...as the old story goes, if I only knew now what I know today....of course I sing much better today. I have more knowledge about singing now, and I've learned how to use it best."

About possible retirement: "I believe in being productive. That's why I will never retire. It's not a question of how long I can go. I think one should always be productive. Retirement is out of the question. That means you are unproductive. What am I trying to prove? If a person has to be productive—survive—he has no alternative. He has to keep going. I think I'm in that position now. I'm supposed to be productive, and I am. I love the road. I love to record. I also love to ski. It's what you want to do. It's called living. I like to work and live."

The 1990's have seen re-issues of many of Al Martino's early albums on CD's. Enjoy yourself, go out and get a few, and listen to a great voice entertain you.

The incomparable Johnny Mathis, 1998. *Chances Are* you will also
find him to be *Wonderful, Wonderful,* although, *It's Not For Me To Say.*
(Photo by David Vance)

JOHNNY MATHIS

The Voice of Romance

True, like Frankie Laine, Johnny Mathis never sang with the bands, but, like Frankie Laine, he came upon the scene too late for the Big Bands and, like Frank, Perry Como, and Tony Bennett, how he could sing. Take his interpretation of just these four songs alone: *Chances Are, A Certain Smile, Wonderful, Wonderful,* and *It's Not for Me to Say* and you have a singing career solidly constructed through Johnny's incomparable phrasing and articulation, not to mention a brilliant microphone technique reminiscent of the early singing innovators Crosby and Como.

On a warm January day in 1998, Johnny Mathis and I sat around his great indoor pool in the Hollywood Hills in Los Angeles, California, in a clearly Southwestern garnished room filled with exotic palms, totems, and cactuses growing in large baskets, among rattan chairs and soft, wide couches, under a high, concaved, box-framed glass ceiling. It has been his home for over 30 years.

"Welcome to my home, Richard, I hope you love it here as much as I do!" Johnny had just returned yesterday from a three-day engagement in Clearwater, Florida. We had been trying to get together for a few months.

No secret, Billboard charts have established Johnny as a world-class romantic singer who has prevailed over 40 years. By some accounts, Johnny Mathis is second only to Frank Sinatra as the most consistently charted albums artist. His *Greatest Hits* spent 490 weeks—count them: nine-and-a—half consistent years on the charts.

Johnny Royce Mathis owes a lot to his dad, Clem Mathis, who fostered his son's career from the time he was a small boy living with his large family in a San Francisco basement apartment. "I learned an appreciation of music from my father who taught me my first songs. He had worked in vaudeville back in the '20s, and always encouraged me and my sisters and brothers to sing."

When Johnny was only 13, his father, realizing his son's exceptional singing ability, took him to see a Bay area voice teacher, Connie Fox, who taught him vocal scales and exercises, voice production, and some operatic skills. "I paid for these lessons by working around Miss Fox's home doing odd jobs, and what little time we had together was very precious and very special. Each day I would take the streetcar from George Washington High School in San Francisco, down to the terminal and then took a train across the Bay and studied with her. We concentrated mainly on voice production. I tried to take more theory, harmony, and piano, but I had so much going on with my athletics. Connie told me that if I learned to produce my tones properly (precise use of diaphragm and vocal chords, and accurate breathing techniques) that I'd probably sing as long as I wanted to. If I ever had an advantage, it was that I learned to sing correctly right from the start so I didn't get sick all the time. Over the years, I probably only canceled two or three performances."

Johnny was very active in school with Student Body President activities as well. "Like any kid, I found time to do everything."

Music was always very special to the young Mathis. He knew that someday he would get involved more seriously, "And, I knew the athletics thing was almost played out because I knew I had gone as far as I could." Unlike his hero, Nat King Cole, the whole singing experience did not come natural to Mathis. "The sound that I have did come naturally, I mean God gives us these little gifts, but Nat, Sarah, and Ella—people like that—they never studied voice in their lives."

Johnny admits he never tried to be different; "I actually tried to copy all the other singers. Nat Cole was my big hero and I think the best singer of all of them. I listened to his music over and over again. Then I listened to Billy Eckstine and Sammy Davis, and then I took all the girl singers like Ella, Peggy Lee, and Lena, of course, and I tried to emulate the high, soft singing that they did. The women have a very flexible sound. I have the advantage of having a big register so I could sing a lot of high and middle range and low notes."

"You mean—like in *Maria*—the closing notes of that song?" I said.

"Exactly—that's amazing that you picked that up...that night after night, year after year, I can still sing that delicate, little high note."

Originally desiring to become an English and physical education teacher, John Royce Mathis enrolled at San Francisco State College. He became "the best all-around athlete to come out of the Bay area," according to local newspaper reports. He set a high jump record only 2 inches short of the Olympic record of the time. Two of his best friends, Bill Russell and Casey Jones, went on to play with the Boston Celtics.

One Sunday afternoon, while singing weekends at the BlackHawk night club, Johnny was spotted by the club's co-owner Helen Noga, who promptly took charge of Johnny's career and who asked Columbia Jazz A & R man George Avakian, who was in the area on vacation, to come to hear Johnny sing at Ann Dee's 440 Club, where she had just booked him.

After listening, Avakian quickly sent this now famous telegram to his record company: "Have found phenomenal 19-year old boy who could go all the way. Send blank contracts."

Although he was invited to participate in the 1956 Olympic trials in Berkeley, California as part of the USA team, his dad encouraged him to forsake it for a recording career. "Good decision, don't you think?" Johnny said.

I guess you would have to say Johnny Mathis is mostly a romantic ballad singer, although he manages to make Christmas carols sound magical, the way they should be interpreted. Nevertheless, he was booked into jazz oriented New York's Blue Angel, Basin Street, and the Village Vanguard. Then, fortunately, Johnny was placed under the management of Columbia's Mitch Miller, who told him to avoid jazz and record pop records. Miller's magic was at work once again. He found *Wonderful, Wonderful* and *It's Not for Me to Say* for the young balladeer.

"The first time I heard my recording of *Wonderful, Wonderful* on the radio, I knew I would become a singer for the rest of my life. I had made the recording about a year before and they took a long time to release it. I had played it myself on my own phonograph, but it wasn't magical until I heard it played on the radio."

"Were you surprised by the phenomenal success of that recording?"

"I was flabbergasted. To this day I am still in awe. I cannot believe that I've had this career, because I did not plan anything."

Although Mitch Miller, the controversial A & R (Artists and Repertoire) man at Columbia Records is sometimes trashed by music critics, I have maintained over and over that he constructed a stable foundation for many of the after Big Band Era non-jazz singers like Frankie Laine, Tony Bennett, Rosemary Clooney, Guy Mitchell, Jerry Vale, as the antidote to the rock and roll music of the time. He helped them establish their careers. "About five or six people in my life—that *had* to be there—if they weren't I don't think that I would be doing what I am doing today. First, My Dad, who introduced me to music, then Helen Noga who discovered me and pushed me. George Avakian, who brought me to Columbia Records, and then there was Mitch Miller, who took over my recording career and taught me literally everything that I know to this day about how to make a record." Johnny maintained that Miller was brilliant, not in an easy way, but more aggressively. Johnny was young, ready and willing to accept—and he needed the strong, positive Miller guidance.

When Johnny chooses a song for a recording, he sets priorities: "The first thing I hear, which is probably what most people hear, is a melody. If it has a pretty melody, I love it. And then, of course, I have to have some literate words to sing. When I go hunting for songs, I usually hunt by composers."

Those two songs were followed by *Chances Are,* a monumental hit of its own, and the most requested song at his concerts right up to today. It was Johnny's first # 1 hit. Another great tune, *The Twelfth of Never,* made it big in 1957. No one who was a teen at the time will forget those recordings. Johnny's rapid vibrato imparted a sentimental, bittersweet quality to that type of love song. He mesmerized his generation.

By 1960, he was voted number one male singer for the year, although he was up against both rock performers Elvis Presley and Ricky Nelson. Johnny does a great job, too, on Artie Shaw's favorite *Begin the Beguine,* Erroll Garner's composition *Misty,* and Henry Mancini's own *Moon River.*

In 1978, Deniece Williams and Johnny recorded a duet album that included the single *Too Much, Too Little, Too Late* that reached number one in 1978, in a time made difficult for balladeers to infiltrate the singles charts, and with his friend Dionne Warwick, he recorded *Friends In Love* that made the Top 40 in 1982. Johnny has also duetted with Gladys Knight; Jane Oliver; his hero's daughter, Natalie Cole, and Nana Mouskouri. When you add it all up, it must be realized that Johnny Mathis' incredible commercial recording success ranks third, just behind Frank Sinatra and Elvis Presley and ahead of the Beatles and the Rolling Stones. Like so many other vocalists of the '50s, '60s, and '70s, Las Vegas became headquarters to many a Mathis headliner concert over the years. Additionally, Johnny went on to perform internationally from Japan to England and back to the White House, where he sang in a Jerome Kern tribute for President and Mrs. Clinton in 1994.

"I've always been proud of my two Grammy nominations, for *Misty* in 1960 and my album salute to the great Duke Ellington in 1992." A fellow Society of Singers member, Johnny has given generously to help other singers in need. Since 1962, he has managed over 50 *Tonite Show* performances. "I think that may be a record, too." he said.

Unlike some singers, Johnny Mathis never sings when he is at home. I couldn't even coax him to utter one note. "I get so tired of hearing the sound of my voice," he said, "that's why I love to sing duets. I grew up singing in a lot of choirs and quartets in school. That's what I really like."

The whole thing with Johnny's success at concerts is preparation. "I make sure that I can sing everything that I have to sing on stage. That gives me the confidence I need. There's no one in the world who had less confidence than I did—I didn't like the way I looked or acted or sang, I was shy and wasn't in command."

Johnny Mathis keeps going strong. What's his secret? I believe it's his consistency to purpose, uncompromising professionalism, great organization, and lots and lots of hard work. "The type of people who like my music are, right across the board, average people who like all kinds of music. They're not musical snobs. It's amazing, I go all over the world to places like Brazil, Germany and France, and it's the same everywhere I go. People that I care to spend any time with seem to like my music."

Johnny Mathis really takes good care of himself these days. He watches his diet and quit drinking alcohol some time ago. He works out five times a week, and the whole process has actually strengthened his voice. "At this point in my life I am really excited to see just how long I can sing at a level that I'm comfortable with. I think I'll be the first one to know when I no longer sound good. Then I'll quit. I'm very careful. I stretch out my performances, and do no more than three days in a row and then I come home for two to three weeks and rest up, play golf, and visit with my friends, like this visit with you."

For up and coming singers, Johnny advises them to get to know their craft and to be very good at what they want to do, if they want success.

Well, Johnny Mathis is still out there singing, and he is proud of what he has done over the years, especially those first recordings that set up his life's work. He appreciates the fact that he succeeded in winning over a large listening audience, people like you readers, who still want to go hear him sing.

Johnny Mathis and I will get together in the Spring of 1998 at Westbury Music Fair on Long Island. I'll be sure to bring along a few copies of this book. He has certainly helped fill some of its pages.

Music Men maker Mitch Miller in his Columbia Records days.
(Richard Grudens Collection)

134

REMEMBERING THE MILLS BROTHERS

With Dan Clemson

On April 29, 1998, Donald Mills will celebrate his 83rd birthday and his 74th year as an entertainer. For the past three years he has served as patriarch of the Mills family in America. On February 25, 1998 The Mills Brothers were honored with a Grammy Lifetime Achievement Award. What a deserved, uplifting honor for this amazing man and his wonderful brothers.

Earlier, on January 1, 1998, I received an encouraging word from Donald Mills' son, John: "I have received your request to interview my father with regards to your book. He will be happy to talk to you next week. Best Wishes." John H. Mills, II. This was a break and a privilege for me since Donald Mills has avoided personal interviews in the last few years.

Donald Mills is the sole survivor of the renowned all-male singing group The Mills Brothers. He continues to pursue his lifelong odyssey as a singer. The Society for the Preservation and Promotion of The Mills Brothers Musical History is the personal passion of founder and editor of *Remembering the Mills Brothers* Newsletter, Dan Clemson. Dan has written much about this first black troupe to break through racial barriers who have gained a mass following in the USA, reaching plateaus never thought possible by any vocal group—let alone black singers.

According to Dan Clemson: "The parents of the four Mills Brothers, John Charles, Herbert Bowles, Harry Flood and Donald Friedlich, were gifted singers. John Mills Sr. sang and managed the Four Knights of Harmony, a traveling barbershop quartet, and Eathel Harrington Mills performed in light opera. The boys sang for pennies in front of

135

**The great Mills Brothers (L to R) Herb, Harry and Don. c. 1960.
(Mills Brothers Society Collection)**

their dad's barbershop when the youngest was seven and the oldest twelve. The influences were certainly there for them, as well as the vocal training acquired from their parents, and the hands-on experience they received as church choir members."

The Four Boys and a Kazoo (a popular tinny, musical toy) started their career at the Mays Opera House in Piqua, Ohio, an event that would alter their musical style and catapult them to fame as a quartet. Stage fright before a large audience and the fact that young John had forgotten the all-important kazoo, the desperate trouper cupped his hands over his mouth and to the surprise of everyone produced sounds far better than that of the tinny kazoo, causing a sensation. What a revelation—what a sound! What an idea!

By now, the boys, John—bass, Herbert—tenor, Harry—baritone, and Donald—lead—added realistic imitations of various musical instruments to their barbershop harmonies. Mastery of the sounds of first, second,and third trumpet, combined with the accompaniment of a $6.25 mail-order guitar played by John, would soon earn them the title of the "human orchestra."

The boys, now with matured voices, impressed programmers at radio station WLW, Cincinnati, and were hired. Within a year, they left and with the help of Duke Ellington and Seger Ellis (the Mills long-time manager), made their way to New York City in 1929, auditioned for CBS radio, and signed a three-year contract with a young, fledging radio executive named William S. Paley. They went from $140.00 a week to $3,250.00 thanks to their radio show and a 14 week engagement at the Palace Theater, where they shared the bill with Bing Crosby, establishing one of the fastest climbs in show business.

Their first recording with Brunswick, *Tiger Rag* and *Nobody's Sweetheart,* reached the top of the charts, becoming the first million-selling record ever by a vocal group. Their unique sound caught the attention of the movie studios, and in 1932 they appeared with Bing Crosby in his first starring film, *The Big Broadcast,* singing *Hold That Tiger.* The film also featured a now legendary cast of greats: George Burns and Gracie Allen, Kate Smith, Cab Calloway, The Boswell Sisters, and The Street Singer—Arthur Tracy. It was the first of their 14 feature film appearances: "We did a lot of cartoons too, you know, the bouncing ball films where we sang the lyrics and everybody in the audience sang along," Donald explained, "It was wonderful going from cartoon to The Mills Brothers."

The boys vocalized their way through *Twenty Million Sweethearts* in 1934, *Broadway Gondolier* in 1935 (with Gary Cooper), *Reveille with Beverly* in 1943, and *When You're Smiling* in 1950. Interesting sidelight: Brunswick printed a disclaimer on every Mills Brothers recording: "No musical instruments or mechanical devices used on this recording other than the guitar," because their special sounds were often mistaken for the real thing.

Shine, with Bing, reached number one in January 1932, the first of a string of Top 10 tunes that year. "*Good-bye Blues,* our theme from the start, was finally recorded in 1932," said Don, "The flipside was *Rockin Chair* with Harry doing a talking bass bridge and me repeating the lyrics on the afterbeat." In 1933, the Mills and Bing Crosby recorded *My Honey's Lovin' Arms* on January 26th. The musical sounds reproduced by those wonderful guys are astounding. It is my preferred Mills Brothers/Bing Crosby recording, also featuring Bunny Berigan on trumpet, Tommy Dorsey on trombone, and Eddie Lang on guitar at the beginning and close of the record. What a collection of talent on one recording. Listen to it carefully.

The Mills Brothers performed with many big bands: *Diga Diga Do* with the great Duke Ellington, *Doin the Low-Down* with the wild Cab Calloway, *In the Shade of the Old Apple Tree* with jazz master Louis Armstrong, "We exhibited our drive and even dared to emulate instruments," Don recalled.

"In 1934, we played London's Palladium and were even invited to appear before King George V and Queen Mary, the first Command Performance ever by black artists. I guess we were the Beatles of the '30s. Harry later loved to tell our audiences that anecdote."

After the death of young John from a lung ailment, the boy's father took his place, literally saving the group from disbanding. He remained rhythmic bass for the next twenty years. The Mills Brothers' career spanned the world, and in 1942 they unearthed an old, unknown song called *Paper Doll.* "When we first heard the song, we didn't like it. So, we worked on it, came up with a new concept and recorded it," Donald remembered, "It was a turning point for us." The recording remained number one for 30 weeks, including 12 weeks on Your Hit Parade radio program.

Other great hits during this period include *Up a Lazy River, You Always Hurt the One You Love, Till Then* and with new lyrics by Johnny Mercer, *Glow-Worm.* When their father retired in 1956, they carried on as a trio, continuing on the club circuit and recording sessions. On Dot Records, they recorded *Get a Job* and *Cab Driver* in 1968.

And, according to Dan Clemson: "By 1981, the boys disbanded after 56 fruitful years. Harry passed away in 1982 and Herbert in 1989. Don and his son, John Hutchinson II, continued on after a brief respite, becoming the fourth generation of Mills family performers. The duo's sounds, to this day, feature a repertory of old Mills Brothers favorites, and are strikingly similar to that of the former trio. But, they would never add a non-family member."

"We considered that way back in 1936 when our brother passed away," Don added, "We tried different guys and it never worked. So, we decided against it, and our father ended up joining us. There are natural harmonies in family groups, a special blend. There are only two of us now, but young John and I are accorded the same standing ovations that the full group received throughout the decades. We flip-flop the harmony parts, just as we used to do, and take turns singing lead."

Henry Miller, now president of General Artists Corporation, has been faithfully booking Mills engagements all over the world for over 50 years. "It's remarkable how the two men achieve the same harmony and beat the original group had," he told me recently.

So, how do they do it? "The simplicity of the songs that we sing makes the audience tap their feet and clap their hands," says Don, "Lyrics you can understand, melodies that are melodic, does it just fine." Of course, you have to add the inimitable Mills' skills.

No one knows how long Donald will continue to sing: "It's been a long, long road. I thought I would be retired by now. But, I enjoy singing; this is my life," Don said. "And I have my son to work with, so everything's going to be just fine."

"The Mills Brothers are the genesis of modern-day black harmony singing," continued Dan Clemson, "They were preceded by a handful of black groups in the style of the traditional camp meeting shouts. The Mills raised the black vocal group from one of novelty status to a commercially accepted form. This singularly unique family fed the dreams of younger black artists and showed them they could reach for the stars.....and touch them." The later accession of Motown groups proves that to be true.

Authors note: Daniel R. Clemson has lived 35 years in Bellefonte, Pa., the ancestral home of the Mills and Clemson families. He has written numerous articles about the Mills Brothers during the last ten years. He chaired the Mills Family Heritage Days in Bellefonte, Pa., that featured Don and John Mills in June 1992, and assisted with the UGHJA Hall of Fame Awards Ceremony in New York City in March of 1993. Dan is a warm and friendly person, and I am overjoyed over his participation in this book.

EDDIE FISHER

Grossinger's Kid Singer Goes Hollywood

I first met Eddie Fisher in the fifties. While in the Army, he was asked to appear on the very first Dean Martin and Jerry Lewis muscular dystrophy telethon at New York's NBC television studio 6B. My job was to admit the talent and document their appearance. Eddie, who was dressed in uniform and accompanied by other Army personnel, talked to me while he was waiting to be ushered on stage. He was very thin and very young. I was also thin and a bit younger.

One of seven children, Philadelphia born Edwin Jack Fisher was brought up in relative poverty. Although the family name was either Tisch or Fisch—Eddie is not sure which—the name Fisher was already adopted by his tyrannical father before Eddie was born in 1928. "We were certainly very poor. But I was lucky. I was born with a voice. Who knows why? Nobody else in the family was musical at all," Eddie said.

When Eddie sang *Santa Claus is Coming to Town* at a school concert, he won first prize, but claims he has no memory of that early performance. He went on to sing in school, churches, and synagogues. "I wanted so much to become a cantor and sing in the temple," he said. The richness and depth of that music had a profound effect on the young singer.

Eddie went through the usual growing pains most singers have experienced on the way up. Al Jolson, Bing Crosby, Jerry Vale, Guy Mitchell—almost everyone. When Eddie received a single ticket to see Perry Como's radio show, Perry asked the audience if anyone wanted to sing. "I found myself jumping out of my seat. He called me up on stage and I sang his own song *Prisoner of Love*. The audience loved it—then Perry said, 'Well, I guess I'll have to sharpen up my barber tools,' with a smile, of course."

141

Music man Eddie Fisher and friend share a smile.
(Movie Star News)

Eddie, by his own admission, is more of a belter than a crooner but, he admired both Frank Sinatra and Bing Crosby, the great crooners of his youth. The first break came when Buddy Morrow was forming his own orchestra and was looking for a band singer. Lester Sacks, of Frank Sinatra's publishing company, auditioned Eddie. Satisfied, Lester, brother of Columbia Record boss Manie Sacks, awarded Eddie the job, opening with the band at the Lincoln Hotel in New York. "I was paid seventy-five bucks a week, and boy, was I excited," Eddie recalled.

Eddie was seventeen and scared. Buddy Morrow (who now fronts the Tommy Dorsey Orchestra) fired him after just three days because Eddie could not keep time or read music. Luckily, Charlie Ventura was in the audience on his last night and hired him to sing with his band at the Boston Post Lodge, a dance hall in Larchmont, New York. Unhappy with Ventura, Eddie received another break, an audition at the famous Copacabana in New York as an opening act for then popular comedian Joe E. Lewis, but beginning in the fall. What a break—and for $125.00 a week. But, first he had to spend the summer practicing his craft as a vocalist with Eddie Ashman's band in the Terrace Room at Grossinger's upstate New York, Catskill Mountain resort. The engagement at the Copa turned out to be that of a disappointing production singer—never singing solos—just doing silly Copa in-house songs with chorus girls.

After some slow breaks, Eddie Fisher was finally "discovered" by popular vaudeville and major radio star Eddie Cantor the following summer while singing at Grossinger's. He toured nationally with Cantor's radio show. Cantor really liked the 21 year old, and Eddie idolized Cantor as one of his life's heroes. "Cantor paid me five-hundred dollars a week, which was a lot of money for someone who had been living on Coke and crackers, and he gave me clothes and an expensive wristwatch."

Thanks to Cantor, when Eddie arrived in Hollywood, he was introduced to the royalty of radio: Jack Benny, Bob Hope, Bing Crosby, George Burns, and Edgar Bergen, but, his really first success came as an opening act for comedian Danny Thomas where his performances brought down the roof at Bill Miller's Riviera in Fort Lee, New Jersey. One of the successful songs was *Thinking of You*. It caused RCA to move quickly to capitalize on the success of Eddie's recording. With help from orchestra leader and arranger Hugo Winterhalter, Eddie

143

recorded *Turn Back the Hands of Time* and *Bring Back the Thrill.* "It was 1950, Richard, and Eddie Fisher had finally made the big-time," Eddie sighed.

The world surely opened up. Eddie was in demand everywhere: the La Vie en Rose Club; the Paramount (with the Mills Brothers); Ed Sullivan's televised *Toast of the Town* variety show; Martin Block's *Make-Believe Ballroom* at radio station WNEW; and with disc jockey Brad Phillips; all in New York. In Philadelphia it was the important Dick Clark Show, and in LA Johnny Grant's popular show. Eddie Fisher was a fast-rising star at just twenty-two.

My affection for Eddie Fisher's singing style arrived when his hit *Oh! My Pa-Pa* hit the airwaves. How I love that recording every time I hear it. It always sounds rich and fresh. Guess it was close to those cantorial songs Eddie always enjoyed singing. He delivers it with belief and heart. "I knew it would be a success," Eddie told me, "although it was pure smaltz, it somehow touched everyone, including my own parents, who at the time thought I sang it just for them."

Eddie returned triumphantly to Grossinger's. "Jennie Grossinger was especially warm to me and as proud of me as if she were my mother, and proud that Grossinger's has been a part of my success. She was a wonderful woman—a lady—simple and dignified. She never forgot a name or a face, never uttered an angry word to anyone. I grew to love her very much." Eddie's records were now selling in the millions. Now the idol of a million teenagers, Edwin Jack Fisher became a private in the United States Army. Discharged in 1953, Eddie was given his own Coca Cola, *Coke Time* TV show televised from the very same studio 6B., which lasted for three very successful years. In those days Dinah Shore sold Chevies, Perry Como sold Chesterfield cigarettes, and Eddie Fisher sold Coca-Cola. "I sure drank enough of it—and I really like the stuff," Eddie said. It was said that kids would order an "Eddie Fisher" instead of saying Coke.

I Need You Now and *Anytime* (another crisp, definitive Fisher recording) as well as *Wish You Were Here* and *Downhearted* were hits for the successful troubadour. Those songs suited him perfectly.

Over the years Eddie Fisher has performed world-wide, including England and Russia. Naturally, he sang at the Cocoanut Grove (Los Angeles), the Empire Room at the Waldorf (New York), the Mocambo

(Los Angeles), and, of course, Las Vegas, where he once starred at Caesar's Palace while his then wife Connie Stevens headlined The Flamingo—just across the street. Eddie has toured the Far East including Vietnam, entertaining the troops, and even traveled with Bob Hope for the USO. He has done it all, and over again.

Everyone knows Eddie was once was married to Debbie Reynolds and Elizabeth Taylor, and it's true that his life was punctuated by a great deal of personal, dramatic adventures beginning with his many affairs and marriages and ending with serious drug problems:

"Drugs had a lot to do with my relationships breaking apart and even starting up in the first place," he admitted, "and I spent too much of my earnings on gambling, and for 60 years I ate junk food. Now, I take care of myself, but Betty Lin (his Chinese-born wife), has helped me through a bout with cancer and years of drug abuse." Eddie declared that if it weren't for Betty Lin, he doubts if he would be around today. After a successful renewal of his life at the Betty Ford Clinic, Eddie now sticks to a fat-free, high-fiber diet and works out every day in his San Francisco apartment.

During the eighties, Eddie was a regular on cruise ships and he says he may even write a sequel to his 1981 autobiography *My Life, My Loves.*

Duke Ellington's vocalist Herb Jeffries sings his immortal song-hit
Flamingo **in the 1940s. (Big Band Jump Collection)**

HERB JEFFRIES

He Arrived by way of Flamingo

Talking to Herb Jeffries is like talking to a long-time friend. Herb is out there working every day of his life and hard to catch up with. "I get up and open my eyes and I'm happy and I am healthy and grateful that there is something for me to do out there everyday, "he said to me one early Monday morning from his beautiful home in the California desert where he likes to carefully observe hummingbirds and similar thrills of nature. "I am trying to write my memoirs," he said, "but I find it hard to sit down for any length of time to write, Richard. I am a nature kind of guy and am more suited to the outdoors."

Herb Jeffries first association with the bands was with Erskine Tate, then Earl Hines, Sidney Bechet, and Blanche Calloway, before becoming a member and now the only remaining survivor of the great Duke Ellington Orchestra of 1941—1943. Some of the legendary instrumental soloists of that band were Ben Webster, Jimmy Blanton, Harry Carney, Juan Tizol, Lawrence Brown, Cootie Williams, Barney Bigard, Johnny Hodges, and Rex Stewart. What a lineup!

Herb was happy to talk about his magnificent singing career: "Singing with America's greatest bandleader and showman was a great stroke of luck for me. I had been making a series of Western movies in Hollywood during the 1930's and was appearing in a film called *The Bronze Buckaroo* in 1940. It was being shown at the Apollo Theater where Ellington was appearing on stage. He introduced me to the audience as *The Bronze Buckaroo,* and it stuck. I did some songs with him, and he hired me on the spot that night. I was making movies, but I knew I'd rather sing with Ellington, so I gave up movies for a while. It was one of the highlights of my life singing with the great genius that was Duke Ellington. Historically, down the road a hundred years or so, it may someday be compared to having played alongside Mozart or

147

Beethoven—yesterdays great composers. I believe Ellington will go down as one of America's great composers. Music was everything to him. He was in love with music, more than anything in the world."

In those days, Herb could imitate any known singer and often would imitate Bing Crosby at rehearsals, "Both Swee' Pea (Billy Strayhorn) and the Duke heard me one night and said, 'Hey, keep that voice—that's the one we want you to use,' they called out to me. Of course, I eventually came into my own and dropped all those voices that weren't my own. But, I also have to tell you that Bing Crosby was my strongest influence. I can still notice the sound of Bing even in my work today."

While Herb was with Ellington, songwriters Ted Grouya and Ed Anderson wrote an interesting, but un-Ellington kind of tune titled *Flamingo.* "When the boys brought the song to Duke one day, he was kinda busy, so he asked me to listen to it and see if I liked it. I did. Duke asked me to pass it over to Swee'Pea (Billy Strayhorn) to arrange. Duke then gave the song a test—like he always did with new songs—right in the theater where we were performing. When the people really showed they liked it, he figured it would sell, so he recorded it."

While in Miami, Herb was so fascinated with the song *Flamingo* that he obtained permission to go to nearby Hialeah to study flamingos in their natural habitat in order to get a feel for interpreting the song. Herb is a warm, emotional singer, always injecting strong feelings into his performances: "You know, Richard, I have always been a bird lover and have owned some exotic birds. Flamingos are very graceful, and, like a flamingo, I would like to fly—you know, like all kids dream of flying—I just want to raise my arms up and fly like a flamingo." Herb's enthusiasm and strong baritone voice sounds like a man half his age.

Flamingo is one of the era's most memorable recordings and certainly Herb Jeffries most durable contribution to the Ellington legacy. I love trying to sing it—in the shower, of course—using the trademark Jeffries' baritone. It's an infectious melody that you can't get out of your head. Tony Martin and others have also done it, but *Flamingo* belongs to Herb Jeffries, just as sure as Tony Bennett owns *I Left My Heart in San Francisco,* Frank Sinatra holds the deed to *My Way,* Kitty Kallen is sole proprietor of *Little Things Mean A Lot,* and Bing holds an iron-clad claim to *White Christmas.*

148

Herb admires his fellow singers: "My friend, Nat Cole, was a great family man, and he never let his ego show in his success. He and I were working joints around Chicago, which was a swinging place during the Chicago World's Fair in 1933 and '34. After hours I would drop in to hear Nat Cole play—he hadn't yet started singing, you know. When he recorded *Nature Boy,* I knew his would turn out to be the best. I also did it *a capella*—during the musicians strike back in '43. It did pretty well, but Nat did it better.

"I always admired my friend and fellow singer Billy Eckstine. Back in Chicago in the early days during the World's Fair we lived in the same hotel and he would practice his horn—driving everybody crazy. He was working in a place called the Club DeLisa and I was playing with Erskine Tate. Tate's band played dance music after basketball games. That's where Earl Fatha Hines first heard me and offered me a job. Billy followed me into the Earl Hines Band. We played the Grand Terrace in the Grand Terrace Orchestra every single night over network radio. He and I both recorded *Skylark*—me first—but Billy ran away with it. It became a big hit for him."

Herb is a longtime friend of Lena Horne: "I first met Lena in New York when she was singing with Teddy Hill's band at the Harlem Opera House....and I was at the Apollo. We met as musicians meet, then she left New York. Years later, we picked up our friendship at an after hours club I opened in California before the war where she would drop by after her work at the movie studios. We had a close relationship then, but she got busy as an actress and I got busy in my career and I lost track of her. We met much later again. She was always the model woman, the kind of woman most men wish they could find; and she is a great singer, especially in the films *Stormy Weather* and *Cabin in the Sky.* I'll always love her."

In 1941 Herb appeared in Duke Ellington's *Jump for Joy* Broadway-style show in Los Angeles. Lasting just three months, it also starred legendary singers Dorothy Dandridge, Ivie Anderson, and blues singer Joe Turner. It produced the songs *Jump for Joy* and *I Got it Bad and That Ain't Good,* two Ellington standards with lyrics by Paul Francis Webster. "The show didn't last too long because there were too many problems with it. It had a lot of backers who wanted to be chiefs and it became difficult. There was a lot of in-fighting about its mes-

149

sage—that Blacks were exploited in Hollywood, and all that stuff of the time. There were always daily changes and it caused too many arguments. But, in the end, it was financial problems that killed it."

Herb Jeffries recording of *Basin Street Blues* is another of his incredible recordings, "I recorded that one with Buddy Baker in 1946— I was a more mature—more independent singer—by that time. It was on Exclusive Records. I was a junior partner with independent producer Leon Renee'. I also recorded *When the Swallows Come Back to Capistrano* which became a hit for me."

And the subject of the intricacy of the song *Lush Life* came up. "I recorded that song as Nat (Cole) also did, and I enjoyed it. You, know," he said, "Swee'Pea (Billy Strayhorn) wrote that song—music and lyrics—when he was only 17 years old. Isn't that amazing? I love that song. It is a mature piece of material. Just stop and listen to it and you will realize what a philosopher Swee' Pea was."

Herb told me that he remains busy doing concerts almost everywhere. When he does jazz or western concerts he reminds his audience that the two musics are interrelated, "Both musics were born in America—Jazz and Western. Neither were borrowed from Europe. Rock has been an important spice to music. There are so many different cultures here—and the musics are merging, that's for sure...but very slowly."

Herb Jeffries latest album is entitled *The Bronze Buckaroo Rides Again,* issued by Warner Brothers. "I signed with Warner four years ago, Richard, doing country western and jazz. I've been making records and doing appearances. The audiences are large. A three day festival draws 50,000 people."

Of the 14 selections, which covers 60 years, you can hear his work from the cowboy films of the thirties, tracks with both Earl Hines and Sidney Bechet, four Ellington numbers including the great *Flamingo* and *Jump for Joy* and live selections from his early appearances at the Apollo.

"Sixty years, Herb," I said, "that's a long time. But what about the '60s, '70s and '80s? Where were you?"

"In Paris," he smiled, "where I had a night club called the Flamingo for ten years." Herb had realized his shifting popularity to Europe in 1950, so he emigrated to France, along with a handful of other jazz expatriates.

Back in the United States Herb Jeffries opened at the Mocambo in Los Angeles, and also worked Ciro's and other night clubs in the area. He moved to Hawaii, living there throughout the seventies where he also toured the clubs and even owned his own nightspot for a while. The eighties found him back in California doing clubwork and taking time to write his memoirs which he titled *Echoes of Eternity,* a sort of auto-biography composed of prose and poetry yet to be published. "I'm now in the editing stage, then I will bring it to fruition, Richard," he explained. "I have been involved in life in many ways over my lifetime. I will be eighty-six in September (1997) and I play three rounds of golf every week, do dozens of charitable shows, and with my wife, Regina, help run our theatrical production business, and I've been a vegetarian for 58 years.

Herb Jeffries is an articulate voice for his music, his inspiring lifestyle, and for the musical hero of his life, the great Duke Ellington. My long conversations with Music Man Herb Jeffries enriched me, generating images of an age gone by filled with great music performed by celebrated musicians and singers. He was one of the distinguished voices.

"Most people arrive on this planet by stork, Richard. I arrived by *Flamingo.*"

A studio shot when Tex Beneke sang *Chattanooga Choo-Choo* with Glenn Miller's orchestra in 1941. (Richard Grudens Collection)

TEX BENEKE

"Pardon Me, Boy, Is that the Chattanooga Choo-Choo?"

It was a genuine thrill talking with Gordon Tex Beneke. The Texas drawl is ever so familiar. The sound of this man's voice means a great deal to me. His singing enriched the personality of the great Glenn Miller Band, especially when vocalizing on *Chattanooga Choo-Choo, I've Got a Gal in Kalamazoo, Jukebox Saturday Night, Don't Sit Under the Apple Tree,* and other memorable Glenn Miller evergreens. True, he's not what you would define as a bona fide vocalist and he did not desire to become a singer, but Glenn Miller drafted him, and Tex was trying to please his new boss so he went along with it. "'You sure can play the tenor (sax), all right, Texas,' he said to me, 'but we need you for some vocals too,'" Tex Beneke told me just today, December 1, 1997, "At first I wasn't sure what he meant."

Tex Beneke wasn't feeling very well today. He's been facing some health problems lately, the discomfort restricting his activities. I found him snuggled up at home with his wife, Sandi, but we had a long conversation anyway about his favorite subject, the vastly celebrated Glenn Miller band and his own inimitable contributions to that legendary musical organization.

On various Miller recordings you could hear Glenn or the Modernaires singing group vamp with words as Tex, whistling, worked himself down from the sax section to the front of the bandstand where he would take up the vocal:

"Hi there, Tex, what'cha say?" Paula Kelly and the Modernaires would sing,

"Step aside partner, it's my day. Bend an ear and listen to my version," and the Modernaires continued, "of a really solid Tennessee excursion," and you know the rest. It's the opening lines to the very first

Gold Record, the immortal *Chattanooga Choo Choo*. Oh, how wonderful it is to hear that 1939 recording spin on the old turntable time after time after time. I never get tired of playing it. So many of us feel the same way.

Gordon Beneke was born in Fort Worth, Texas in 1914. Playing sax since he was nine years old, he began playing in local territory bands. Gordon joined the Ben Young Band and toured from Texas to Ohio. "In Detroit, I got this call from a guy by the name of Glenn Miller. I didn't know who he was at the time. He was starting a new band, and Gene Krupa recommended me because he had heard me in Young's band one night when he was scouting local bands for personnel for his band. Glenn wanted to know if I were interested. He offered me $50.00 a week, the same as everybody would be making to start, and would build on from there. I hesitated and asked him for $52.50 so I could be the highest paid member. Dead silence—Glenn was frugal, you know—'O.K.,' he said,' but you'll have to prove yourself.'" Gordon drove his 1936 Plymouth for twenty-four hours through the snow to his first rehearsal. "When it came time for me to take a vocal on a song called *Doin' the Jive*—Glenn sang 'Hi, there, Tex, what'cha say?' That's when the whole business of calling me Tex began. I guess he liked that Texas drawl. Now only people from my old home town ever call me Gordon."

After a favorable beginning at the Glen Island Casino in New Rochelle, New York, The Glenn Miller band went off on a national tour. "We were all young and didn't mind traveling," Tex said, "People would come from hundreds of miles away to hear us play. We'd perform at theaters, barns, parks, dance halls, and (dance) pavilions. We didn't know we were making history. We were just enjoying ourselves and making a living."

Tex Beneke quickly became a valuable commercial personality for Glenn's band. Glenn never missed an opportunity to feature Tex playing and vocalizing on specialty tunes. Tex was always cast into the spotlight and the public loved him. He found it difficult to learn lyrics but could learn anything on the sax if he heard it just once.

"It's ironic, Richard," Tex continued, "I really didn't like most of those tunes I sang including *Chattanooga Choo-Choo*. All I was interested in was playing my sax. Of course, I had to go along with the vocal in order to be accepted. I had to do what Glenn wanted. That was part of

154

the deal. Finally he put me doing parts with the Modernaires vocal group."

Tex was destined to become somewhat of a singer. He first thought *Chattanooga Choo Choo* was a dog and would not get off the ground: "But every time we played and sang it the roof would come off the place. I really didn't care about singing. All I considered myself to be was a poor man's Johnny Mercer. I always steer clear of it until I have to sing on some of the jobs when I'm leading my own orchestra. The folks want to hear those favorites, you know. I had to keep some of those arrangements to please the folks, especially the ones that made it big."

The movie *Sun Valley Serenade,* featuring *Chattanooga Choo Choo, It Happened in Sun Valley* with Tex and the Modernaires, and *I Know Why* (And So Do You) and *In the Mood,* catapulted the Glenn Miller Band and Tex Beneke into the big time. It was their first film, a lighthearted comedy that also starred internationally famous ice skating star Sonja Henie, John Payne, Lynn Bari, comedian Milton Berle, the amazing dancing of the superb Nicholas Brothers and Dorothy Dandridge, and Glenn's entire band. The second film, *Orchestra Wives,* with George Montgomery, Cesar Romero, and comedian Jackie Gleason featured the Mack Gordon and Harry Warren score, the biggest Miller hits ever, *At Last, Serenade in Blue* (with that beautiful opening passage arranged in thirty minutes by arranger Billy May), and Tex Beneke singing *I've Got a Gal in Kalamazoo.* The great Glenn Miller Band with Tex Beneke was established forever.

According to George Simon, author of the definitive book *Glenn Miller,* band members always said that Tex was a gentleman and a generous friend to everyone, adding warmth and wholesomeness to the band.

As is well-known, after Glenn disappeared over the English Channel in 1944, Tex took over the band. "I was asked by Mrs. (Helen) Miller if I would front the Air Force Band in 1946. We broke the record at the Hollywood Palladium in 1947. We had 6,750 people dancing on opening night. The Miller name was just magic. I kept the job until 1950, when I decided to form my own band. I called it the Tex Beneke Orchestra. We played to capacity audiences everywhere. In New York, we played the Paramount, the Pennsylvania Hotel and lots of shows at

Tex Beneke's brand new 1946 band with the Moonlight Serenaders on the Chesterfield Supper Club. (Ed Burke photo)

Disneyland in California. We called our music *The Music Made Famous By Glenn Miller* right into the 1980's." Tex and his band has played right up to recently. Patty Andrews was a frequent guest as were some of the original Miller personnel including vocalist Ray Eberle and current versions of the Modernaires singing group. "I always found it comfortable singing with Tex and his guys," Patty Andrews told me recently.

"Today, Richard, we do engagements mostly at private parties, which are not open to the public. Sometimes at the Elk's Club or at night clubs and theaters. Looking back—all I can ever think about—that special place in my heart—is that the Glenn Miller Orchestra itself that was the highlight of my career. Just to be able to work with a man like Glenn,, somebody who knew exactly what he wanted and worked hard enough to get it. He was a fine arranger, a good lead trombone player, and an excellent person, someone to look up to always. He also made a singer out of me—that was something in itself."

No *if,* ands, or *buts,* Tex Beneke was an important singing, non-singer of the Big Band Era.

Richard Grudens talks to WLIM's Bob Stern.
Bob is a Glenn Miller/Tex Beneke aficionado.

157

**Philadelphia's newest music man Lou Lanza.
"Hope you like the photo, Richard."
(Richard Grudens Collection)**

LOU LANZA

New Guy on the Block From Philly

He caught the corner of my eye from a distance. Philadelphia has already digested and documented his music, and my friend, music critic Anthony DiFlorio III, was able to pin-point his exact location for me: Fairless Hills, Pennsylvania, in a neat, new twin-style house with his wife Maria, two cats, Scat and Bijou, and a well-tuned piano.

Lou Lanza (not a stage name) was just the guy this book was searching for, and, no, he is not related to Mario Lanza, whose name was not really Lanza anyway. Articulate and intelligent, Lou will be twenty-eight in July.

Take note, *Music Men* fans. Singing Sinatra, Torme, and maybe a little Feinstein, Lou Lanza will sometimes evoke the sounds of John Birks Gillespie himself. His two albums, *Corner Pocket* and *The Road Not Taken,* are both trips down memory lane and glances into the future. Who else do you know who can smooth over Rodgers and Hart's *My Funny Valentine* to his dad's and uncle's unusual arrangement with crying violin and viola; beautifully scat through Dave Frishberg and Bob Dorough's *I'm Hip,* and bop over *A Night In Tunisia,* emulating three different singers doing three different gigs? And, when you're sure you know him, he turns around and deals a little Rap, too!

Ideas come alive when you talk with Lou Lanza. We sat down on this beautiful day in January of 1998 to talk music. He is very serious about his career.

"I learned from Sinatra," Lou began, "especially his early Dorsey days and the later Columbia stuff. I sang along with Sinatra each day, trying to learn the craft." Sid Mark, a well-known disc jockey on WWDB in Philly, who has played Sinatra recordings over his forty-year career with shows named *Friday with Frank* or *Saturday Sounds with Sinatra,* influenced the young Lanza. Lou wanted first to be a baseball player and was once scouted by the Philadelphia Phillies. "I was a pretty good center fielder and had a great ability to generate bat power into the gaps." But, singing his own songs took over his life. Lou's family is all musical. His dad, Louis Lanza Jr. is a violinist with the Philadelphia Orchestra, his Uncle, Joseph Lanza, plays the viola, and his son, Joseph Lanza Jr., is concert-master of the London Ontario Orchestra in Canada. His mom, Joan Trombetta-Lanza, is a classical singer and organist, and her brother Vince is a musical arranger and director.

Lou Lanza really sings for his supper. During the day he does weddings, masses, and funerals, and at night does gigs around Philly (like J.J.'s Grotto with his fellow jazz musicians) and, of course, performs nationally, recently completing a gig at New York's elegant Tavern—On-The Green, his debut in the Big Apple, and at the Los Angeles Cine' Grill in the Hollywood Hotel.

"In 1993, after finishing singing at a funeral, the closing selection *Amazing Grace*—in an arrangement that goes up and up and up—like Bobby Darin's *Mack the Knife* arrangement—it emotionally affected an attending Washington, D.C. businessman, Joseph Narducci, who approached me afterwards. It was like an MGM musical miracle. We spoke for a while and he wondered why I wasn't more well-known and offered to finance what became my first CD, *The Road Not Taken*. It was a miracle jumpstart for me."

That CD spawned some very good Lanza selections, especially that version of *My Funny Valentine* I mentioned earlier and Ira Gershwin and Kurt Weill's great tune *My Ship*. "I am very careful when I chose my CD selections. Right now I am choosing songs for my new CD which will be produced by Challenge Records, a Holland (European) company. They want me to do mostly ballads, maybe with an off-beat style. They feel my strong suit is a no-swing ballad. But, I was trained in musical theater so I always stress the lyric of a song. (Some say his performance as Sky Masterson in his St.Joseph's Prep High School production of *Guys and Dolls* was memorable). I try to offer it in a different way. If a song doesn't move me—if I don't feel right about it—I just won't do it...I can't do it. Take *How High the Moon*—Ella, of course, did it best—but, I can't fake it. The lyrics are great, but the song doesn't move me emotionally—I tried to do it in an innovative way, but I just can't. I think an audience can detect that."

Lou was fortunate to be taught his craft by the famous voice teacher, the late Carlo Menotti, who also coached Tony Bennett, Frankie Avalon, Liza Minelli, Laura Branigan and others. "He believed that you had to take care of your voice—but not to baby your voice—your vocal chords, "Lou explained while his two cats purred by his side, "and that you had to train as though you were training for a voice marathon, pacing yourself, getting stronger, lasting longer, perhaps for the days you have to do three—four—or maybe up to six shows a day."

One of the numbers Lou is considering for the forthcoming album is a Harold Arlen/Truman Capote little-known song entitled *Don't Like Goodbyes* from the 1954 Broadway show *House of Flowers*. With phrases like—"Don't want to leave you, don't want to grieve you"—the tune fits Lou perfectly. Lou played and sang the full version for me. He skillfully stretches the lyric and bends it, then arrives back on track, sounding a lot like Billie Holiday would on such a song, one of the most beautifully written songs ever heard in the theater. It was indeed a treat to listen to him first-hand. Lou's professionalism took over, his impeccable phrasing reminiscent of the young Nat Cole, whom he reveres, as he does Tony Bennett, Johnny Hartman, Mel Tormé, and Chet Baker. "I also like Harold Arlen's *Get Happy*, but I do it in F-Minor which makes it a dark and more hip arrangement."

He puts his piano to work allowing him to learn both music and lyrics through practice at home. "If I have to re-work a vocal, even though I am isolated from musicians, I am able to continue after rehearsal sessions. I can perfect passages or pace myself. Being able to play as well as sing is a definite advantage."

Lou Lanza confesses to singing all day as Bing Crosby did. "I love singing, so I sing. It helps my voice strength to sing, so I sing. That's what I do. When I performed in off—Broadway version shows like *West Side Story, Grease,* or *The Fantasticks,* I sang all day to keep my voice strong and practiced. You get better with practice, that's for sure. I wish I had two more hours in the day, to get to some of the other songs I'm not quite ready to do yet in public," he said with a yearning.

Now, after all this, you simply must realize Lou Lanza is not yet twenty-eight, but he is acutely aware of what he must do to achieve his goal of a successful singing career. He speaks with authority on his subject. Even at this young age, he has done it all. Being from a musical family has contributed. Singing in clubs with a blend of classical and jazz musicians has added to his stature. Lou has proven himself and continues to persevere. With the help of composers Harold Arlen, George Gershwin, Lorenz Hart and Richard Rodgers, Johnny Mercer, Neal Hefti, and even Dizzy Gillespie, not to mention the select musicans and arrangers, Lou Lanza is definitely carrying the torch into the future.

Singer, actor, walking musical encyclopedia, Philadelphia singer Lou Lanza is definitely on the right road. You can tell. It's the talent of young vocalists like Lanza that keeps the music going.

SOME OTHER SINGERS YOU KNOW

VIC DAMONE—Still Breaking Hearts

Vito Rocco Farinola, known to all as Vic Damone—the guy who Sinatra claims, "...has the best set of pipes in the business," celebrated 50 years in the singing business in 1997 and performed at a sold-out one-man Carnegie Hall concert on January 24, 1998. Afterwards, his publicist Rob Wilcox told me the show was a terrific success. Vic worked as an usher at the New York Paramount Theater when he was a kid and became influenced by singers like Frank Sinatra. Vic's voice, although clear as a bell, was similar to Sinatra's style and voice tone in his early period, especially on his 1946 radio air-checks *You Go To My Head* and *All Through the Day,* Sinatra songs Vic performed on station WHN.

" Most songs have been recorded by Frank Sinatra," Vic said, "but you have to try to give them a new interpretation." Vic cheerfully admits the emulation was deliberate at the time, "I tried to mimic him. My training, my learning process was watching performers onstage. I decided that if I could sound like Frank, maybe I did have a chance."

For me, Vic Damone's most appealing recording was *You're Breaking My Heart,* which will always be his song as Tony Bennett's is *I Left My Heart in San Francisco.* Vic, of course, did not come up with the Big Bands, but he appeared in a movie, The Strip, with the great Louis Armstrong, Jack Teagarden, and Earl Hines. In the 1955 film *Hit the Deck,* Vic sang Vincent Youmans' wonderful song *Sometimes I'm Happy,* and my friend, arranger/conductor Frank De Vol directed Vic singing *An Affair To Remember,* the title song from the 1957 hit movie.

Vic sometimes avoids those old tunes in his current work, but always does Lerner and Loewe's classic *On The Street Where You Live,* from the Broadway musical *My Fair Lady,* for my money the definitive recording of that song. Vic toured with Bob Hope's USO troup at Chu Lai, Vietnam in 1966. When they were up in a plane as they approached

Vic Damone in his Metro-Goldwyn Mayer movie days.
(Movie Star News)

Pleiku, home of the 4th Infantry Division, Vic asked Bob, "What are those puffs of smoke down there? Artillery fire?" and Bob answered, "No, they're just burning General Charles De Gaulle's photograph."

Vic kinda retired for a while then appeared back on the scene in the early eighties, mostly because of a renaissance he enjoyed in England. It seems a DJ, BBC's David Jacobs, gave Vic a lot of play, especially on his 1961 album *The Pleasure of Her Company*. Vic toured the British Isles to standing room audiences during the eighties. "When he walked on stage, before he sung a note, he received a standing ovation every-time, everywhere," said Denis Brown of The Dick Haymes Society in a recent society newsletter. In 1996, twenty-five of Vic's Mercury Recordings was reissued under the title, *The Mercury Years.*

Vic Damone appeared onstage as Sky Masterson at Westbury Music Fair in a revival of the 1940's Broadway musical *Guys and Dolls.* Over the years he has performed regularly at Michael's Pub and Rainbow and Stars in New York, and in important venues in Las Vegas and Atlantic City.

Some people say Vic Damone hates show business, "But, I'm never tired of singing," he says emphatically. Luckily, *Reader's Digest* had issued *The Legendary Vic Damone* quality CD with 30 new and 30 old recordings. I like that.

JACK JONES—There's Always Been a Song in the Air

I like Jack Jones. I also like his dad, Allan Jones, who was a great, popular light classical singer back in the '30s, appearing in a couple of Marx Brothers films *A Night At the Opera* and *A Day at the Races,* as well as in an operetta entitled *The Firefly* with Jeanette McDonald. His great song was *The Donkey Serenade.* Jack's mom was actress Irene Hervey.

Jack Jones is a chip off the old block, as they say. He started, like so many others, imitating the then acceptable sound of Frank Sinatra. However, his engaging style and pleasant voice led him to success during the 1960's, when he recorded *Lollipops and Roses* and *Call Me Irresponsible.* Between 1962 and 1968, Jack had twenty successful recordings on the charts. His biggest hits were *Wives and Lovers* in 1963 and *The Race Is On* in 1965.

165

Jack Jones' two 1960's albums, *The Impossible Dream* and *Dear Heart,* were re-issued in 1985 on MCA Records. Jack won two Grammys, one in 1962 and the other in 1964. Jack has also toured with Bob Hope's Christmas USO troup in the 1960's. They played at Tan Son Nhut, Vietnam during the Christmas holidays in 1965.

STEVE LAWRENCE—A Musical Permanent Bond

Steve Lawrence first found success on Steve Allen's original Tonight Show on NBC television in New York. It's also where Steve first met another young singer, Eydie Gorme'. After some time on Steve's show, they married in 1957 in Las Vegas at the El Rancho where they were the opening act for Joe E. Lewis. "Joey showed up wearing Chinese pajamas and a yarmulke. He was crazy," Steve said. Like a lot of his contemporaries, Steve sounds a lot like Frank Sinatra too. Sometimes, when I hear him on New York's WQEW, I swear it's Sinatra. Then his own recognizable sounds come through later in the recording. However, Steve's recordings *Portrait of My Love* and *Go Away Little Girl* are distinctly his own.

Steve and Eydie perform together, *Forever,* **in Las Vegas.**
(Movie Star News)

Born Sidney Leibowitz in Brooklyn, New York, in 1935, Steve also became a Broadway performer. He appeared in *What Makes Sammy Run?* in 1964. "I spent two years of my life in that show. Doing Broadway was very important to me. I auditioned for the part three times— and they finally gave me the job—in Philly, "Steve said while being recently interviewed on television," Abe Burrows directed and Bob Alda and Barry Newman were in it. It won the Drama Critics Award in New York. A singer has to work where ever he can. "

Steve recorded *I Gotta Be Me,* "I recorded it first, before Sammy (Davis) did it. Eydie and I told Sammy to record it too, because we felt he would do it even better. He did. His is the best version."

In 1991, Steve and Eydie toured with Frank Sinatra during his Diamond Jubilee Tour. He always sings *More,* one of his signature tunes, during his tours. The couple duets on songs like *Baby It's Cold Outside* and *Our Love is Here to Stay,* trading off songs, singing counterpoint and finishing each other's vocal punchlines.

Steve is known to perform a little slapstick humor when in concert. Some fans like it and some don't. It's Steve, and it's all right with me. "I notice a lot of young people coming to our concerts," Steve says, "When young people hear Gershwin and Arlen for the first time, it's new songs to them. They will ask who wrote this or that song. I tell them good is good." For thirty-five years Steve and Eydie have traveled the world, and at Westbury Music Fair, like many other venues, they are almost always sold out soon after the show's announcement. Not many can accomplish that. Steve and Eydie (like peanut butter and jelly) compliment one another and always have. They had their own TV show for a while beginning in 1959, and Steve had his own show in 1965. Orchestra leader and arranger Billy May told me he loved working with Steve and Eydie. So did Steve Allen. Steve's funny. He's no Jerry Seinfeld, but his songs will always be enjoyed.

LOU RAWLS—Soulful Sounds

Soulful, popular Lou Rawls, reared in Gospel singing and influenced by Ray Charles, hails from Chicago where he was born in 1935. His first album, *Lou Rawls* in 1962, was a terrific first start. A 1967 Grammy winner, Lou Rawls had signed a contract with Capitol Records five years before. In 1958, after military service, Lou, while traveling with singer Sam Cooke, was involved in a car crash and almost killed. Never a band singer, Lou consistently sang Big Band things. A prolific album maker, Lou's recordings were always in the top twenty and higher. In the 1970's he switched to the MGM label with a winning title *A Natural Man*. His seventh LP became a number two hit with *You'll Never Find Another Love like Mine*. Lou is also a film actor and a popular Las Vegas attraction, as well as a television performer.

BILL FARRELL—Where There's Hope, There's Farrell.

Big **Bill Farrell** is a product of Cleveland, Ohio. In 1947 at the Chez Ami in Buffalo, New York, Bob Hope walked in, liked what he heard and took vocalist **Bill Farrell** to Hollywood. **Bill** went on to sing on Bob's radio show that featured young Doris Day and Les Brown's Orchestra. He traveled to Germany on the next Hope Christmas Show. Bill sings with heart and soul: "I try to express a song the way I think a man would sing," says Bill, who now lives in California and is singing better than ever. Bill may be one of the most underrated vocalists ever.

PAT BOONE—No More Mr. Nice Guy?

A descendant of Daniel Boone, Charles Eugene Boone first saw light in Jacksonville, Florida, 62 years ago. His parents wanted a daughter they were going to name Patricia, thus they called him Pat. So, okay, he never sang with the bands, but he sure sang his head off for all the following years. He meandered into the singing business via *Ted Mack's Original Amateur Hour* (The *Star Search* of its day) and *Arthur Godfrey's Talent Scouts*. *Two Hearts, Two Kisses, One Love* was his first hit in 1954. *Ain't That a Shame* was second. We all know the tremendous success of *Love Letters in the Sand* that remained on the charts for 34 weeks. Add *Moody River, April Love,* and *Friendly Persuasion*—well, you know what I mean. Pat enjoyed my first book, *The Best Damn Trumpet Player*. "I know what's involved and I really salute you," he wrote.

Pat also holds the all-time *Billboard Magazine* record of 200 consecutive weeks on the charts with more than one song.

Pat Boone is a friendly, spiritual guy with an ideal family and 15 grandchildren. Being neighbors, Rosemary Clooney's son Gabriel married Pat's daughter Debbie (who also had a tremendous hit with *You Light Up My Life*). The last time I checked on Pat he was not wearing his white bucks but had traded them in for a heavy metal outfit and was singing Ozzy Osbourne's *Crazy Train*. (He was only kidding, of course).

JIMMY ROSELLI—A True Italian Troubadour

One song alone would certify the above fact. *When Your Old Wedding Ring was New:* "That recording changed Jimmy's life. The long hard hours of playing small clubs and receiving low pay were finally paying off," wrote Anthony DiFlorio III in an article written in 1996. "When he gets out in front of the spotlight, he gives his all—every minute with every song." And, Don Cornell recently told me that Jimmy is "the best Italian singer around." I know Jimmy sells out at Westbury Music Fair on Long Island and in Atlantic City venues like Caesars, everytime he appears.

It was on December 26, 1925 when Jimmy found first light in Hoboken, New Jersey. He lost his mother the next day, and Grandfather "Papa" Roselli raised him, instilling much love and an appreciation of music in the young man. He began singing in church choirs and later at the Gay Ninties Room at the local Meyers Hotel. Jimmy was a first-prize winner at a Major Bowes Amateur Hour show, the same place where Frank Sinatra got his first break.

The Second World War summoned Jimmy for a stint in Army. His need to sing even then was fulfilled on radio from Linz, Austria, while traveling with the 42nd Rainbow Division Band. After being discharged in 1946, Jimmy took singing lessons and went on to perform throughout the east coast where he became a great favorite, thanks in part to assistance from the great Jimmy Durante in 1954. The lovable, popular Durante, a singer in his own right, encouraged him and solicited the management of the famed Latin Quarter nightclub in New York City to raise his salary and extend his engagement. Jimmy went on to play all the big clubs in and around New York, including a major appearance at the Copacabana in 1964 (with a response so fantastic that the manage-

"Jimmy Roselli is the best Italian singer" says fellow performer Don Cornell.

ment extended his four-week engagement to a five-year contract), Palumbo's in Philadelphia, and later at Carnegie Hall.

Mala Femmina (as arranged by Ralph Burns), *Pal of My Cradle Days, This Heart of Mine,* and *Come Into My Heart* are some of Jimmy Roselli's best recordings that still endear him to millions. Listen for Jimmy's new hit *What is a Song* when you catch his next performance. He tells the answer.

ANDY WILLIAMS: Williams Brothers Lead Singer Goes Solo

One of the better high baritones (Vic Damone and Jack Jones are the others), Howard Andrew Williams, born on December 3, 1930 in Wall Lake, Iowa, has had a long run as a single after separating from singing with the Williams Brothers (with Kay Thompson) and beginning a solo career with appearances on Steve Allen's TV show. "I've

Andy Williams performs at Branson, Missouri (Photo by Jim Lersch)

never heard Andy sing a dumb song. He always does good material," Steve once said.

Andy, when very young, worked for the movies using his voice for dubbing. Andy also appeared in Bing Crosby's movie *Going My Way* as one of the choir of young boys singing *Swinging On a Star.*

He has traveled overseas with Bob Hope's troupe to entertain the troops and has appeared on many Bob Hope specials and tributes. *Born Free, Moon River, Hawaiian Wedding Song, Dear Heart,* and *A Summer Place* are some of Andy's, as they say, greatest hits. I call them tender favorites because Andy sings that way. Andy does most of his singing in Branson, Missouri, these days where he owns a hotel and where the Lennon Sisters hang out.

AUTHOR'S NOTE: Frankie Laine, Tony Bennett, Billy Eckstine, Tom Postilio, and Perry Como were profiled in my first book, The Best Damn Trumpet Player in 1997.

MORE GUYS WHO SANG
WITH THE BANDS

EDDY HOWARD—To Each His Own, He Found His Own.

Eddy was another musician/singer band leader, recording songs like *It's All in the Game, Old Fashioned Love, Can't We Talk it Over,* and *When My Dreamboat Comes Home.* His orchestra started in 1942. Eddie was the boy singer. He had a way with a song and a way with an audience. He earlier recorded his theme song *Careless* (which he wrote) with Dick Jurgens' band which turned out to be one of his most popular recordings. Eddy played both guitar and trombone. His best known recording was, of course, *To Each His Own.* In 1962-63, after the demise of the Big Band Era, Eddy Howard returned to gigs on Catalina Island, off the coast of California, performing with a small group during the summertime until his accidentally premature death in 1963 at his home in Palm Springs, California.

BILLY ECKSTINE—Romantic Balladeer.

I once spent an entire evening with Billy Eckstine backstage at Westbury Music Fair in the mid 1980's. During our interview, his old friend John Birks (Dizzy) Gillespie dropped in on us. I covered this infamous meeting in my first book, *The Best Damn Trumpet Player.* Billy, Dizzy, William B. Williams, and my photographer Camille Smith had a great time exchanging big band stories. Billy's warm baritone voice was always one of my favorites. *Fools Rush In* and *Everything I Have is Yours,* as well as his rendition of *Caravan,* are among his best-known recordings. He was responsible for the careers of both Sarah Vaughan and Fran Warren, whom he helped immeasurably along their way. Billy held the distinction of being the first Black singer to grace the cover of *Life Magazine.*

Billy Eckstine and Richard Grudens 1984. (Photo by C. Camille Smith)

He began it all at an amateur show imitating the voice of Cotton Club star Cab Calloway. That earned him a spot in Earl Fatha Hines' Grand Terrace Orchestra. In Billy's own first band, Dizzy Gillespie, Sarah Vaughan, Miles Davis, Charlie Parker, Art Blakey, and Gene Ammons were all players, as was an old friend of mine Budd Johnson, the fine musician and arranger, whose music life I also profiled in *The Best Damn Trumpet Player*. Budd helped to put the band together. What a lineup of talent.

After my somewhat tumultuous and funny interview with Billy Eckstine, the first well-known singer I interviewed, all the rest of my interviews seemed easier. The vivid recollection of his no-nonsense point of view about life and music and his great, romantic voice will always occupy part of my memory.

BOB CARROLL—Singing Gentlemen, Fine Actor.

A resident of Port Washington, New York, when he passed away in 1995, Bob Carroll began his singing career with the Charlie Barnet band when Lena Horne was Barnet's girl singer. His marvelous baritone voice was also heard in the bands of Jimmy Dorsey and Glenn Miller (Army Air Force Band). Some said he was a Crosby imitator. If he was, he did it better than anyone, according to Will Friedwald in his book *Jazz Singing*. Then, as an accomplished actor, his best known role was his portrayal of Tevye in the national tour of *Fiddler on the Roof* in the '70s. Bob also appeared on television with Steve Allen, Jackie Gleason, and Johnny Carson. His Broadway credits were *Fiorello* (as Mayor LaGuardia), *La Cage aux Folles,* and *Shenandoah.* Bob appeared frequently with the Los Angeles Philharmonic as baritone soloist.

I spoke to Bob's wife Nadine recently. She spoke of his other achievements over a long and successful career. "Bob appeared in concert with his good friend Skitch Henderson and the New York Pops at Carnegie Hall. Bob was semi-retired in recent years," she added, "and made so many benefit performances for the Actors Home in New Jersey and frequently volunteered at St. Francis Hospital in Roslyn (New York). Our son Keith and our four daughters, Jody, Laura, Melanie, and Chris, as well as his 10 grandchildren, were very proud of him."

JOHNNY MERCER—A Man Bursting with Talent, Was Also a Singer.

My friend, Song Star Margaret Whiting once said that prolific songwriter Johnny Mercer was a man bursting with talent and always looking for a place to channel his energies. "Johnny, an out-of-work actor, passed a sign outside a theater that said LYRICS WANTED. He went in and found both his profession and his wife, Ginger, who was a dancer in the chorus," she said. Mercer went to Hollywood, worked with Hoagy Carmichael on *Lazybones,* returned to New York, worked with Paul Whiteman and later, on the radio with Benny Goodman, where he wrote a song a week.

With Glenn Wallich he formed Capitol Records. Their second release was Ella Mae Morse and Freddie Slack's band doing *Cow-Cow Boogie* which sold 25,000 copies in the first week. Capitol was responsible for advancing the singing careers of Nat Cole, Jo Stafford, Peggy Lee and Margaret Whiting. But Johnny was also a singer. Among his recordings are his own *Mr. Meadowlark* (with Bing Crosby), *Personali-*

**Margaret Whiting sent me this priceless photo
with composer, lyricist and singer Johnny Mercer.
(Margaret Whiting Collection)**

ty, Candy, (the latter two written by others), and his *Ac-Cent-Tchu-Ate
the Positive, G.I.Jive, Glow Worm, On the Atchison, Topeka,* and the
Santa Fe, and a lot of other songs written by himself and others.

Johnny Mercer's southern drawl and warm, good-natured style
made him a natural, singing on radio in the 1940's. I loved him best
when he sang his own composition, *Small Fry.*

"He once told me, 'Grow up, kid,'" Margaret recalled. After all,
Margaret knew him well and was a protégé. "It was the best advice I
ever received." Margaret Whiting loved Johnny Mercer, her mentor, her
hero. For me he was a great song writer, and a not-so-bad singer. Dedicated to musical excellence, Johnny Mercer's policy reflected his
approach to all his work, whether writing or singing.

VAUGHN MONROE—He Was Racing With the Moon.

I remember huddling in doorways of narrow-front record shops
along New York's Forty-second street during the winter of 1948, where

175

outside were mounted harsh-sounding speakers blaring Vaughn Monroe's wonderful recordings of *Ballerina* and *Ghost Riders in the Sky.* One of those days I looked up and there was a figure of Vaughn Monroe beaming high above the marquee' outside the Strand Theater, which boasted his name in lights. Inside, when the movie ended, the lights came up, and Vaughn's formidable great band broke out with his theme *Racing with the Moon,* as the great stage rose up from the orchestra pit. An old Long Island friend of mine, Bob Incagliato, was a great fan of Vaughn Monroe. Like me and others, Bob found the husky voice of Monroe, especially on recordings like *Riders in the Sky,* a great compliment to the song itself. "Other versions weaken the song's strong message," Bob said, "Monroe's delivery and voice power move the song along and make a mythical legend almost believable."

Born in 1911 in Akron, Ohio, Vaughn played in the school band and won the State Trumpet Championship at 14 years old. This allowed him

Singer bandleader Vaughn Monroe, 1955. (Richard Grudens Collection)

to go to Milwaukee and play under the direction of famed band conductor and composer John Philip Sousa, inspiring Vaughn to become a band leader. He first recorded his voice with Larry Funk's band singing *Rain* and *Too Beautiful for Words.*

After stints in other bands, Vaughn organized his own band, and my friend, the prestigious band booker of the agency named after him, Willard Alexander, booked him, bringing him to the attention of RCA, where he recorded for years and wound up as their spokesman. His first important gig was playing the New York Paramount, singing his theme *Racing with the Moon* for the first time, which he wrote with arranger John Watson. Adding a string section to the band, he toured nationwide, eventually opening a large dinner theater/restaurant in Framingham, Mass. He sang on his own show, *The Camel Caravan,* and appeared in western movies. Vaughn continued to record even after he disbanded his orchestra in 1953. Remember *Sound-Off, There I've Said It Again?* Both were immense hits.

BOB EBERLY AND RAY EBERLE—The Bob & Ray of Good Music.

Both handsome, romantic baritones, the Eberle/Eberly brothers sang with the top bands of the era. Bob vocalized with Jimmy Dorsey, notably on those very successful Tutti Camarata arranged duets with Helen O'Connell *(Tangerine, Green Eyes),* and Kitty Kallen *(Besame' Mucho).*

Bob spelled his name ending in a *Y,* whereas Ray ended his with an *E,* in order to distinguish one brother from another. The correct family spelling was Eberle. "Helen (O'Connell) had a crush on Bob," Margaret Whiting, recalled recently, "He was so nice to her on those band bus trips. He taught her how to comfortably sleep on a bus—he would bring her a blanket—or some pillows." Margaret toured with Helen for a while in the 1980's with Four Girls Four that included Rosemary Clooney and Rosemarie (and alternately Kay Starr).

"He sort of took care of me," Helen told me some time ago. "If Bob had gone off as a single, I wonder how successful he would have been? Would he have been as successful as Sinatra or Haymes?"

Bob Eberly at the mike with Jimmy Dorsey's band, 1941. (Jack Ellsworth Collection)

"Bob Eberly was bigger than all of us," said Dick Haymes to writer and broadcaster Fred Hall in his book *Dialogues In Swing,* "you know, with Jimmy Dorsey. I mean, when he was singing *Amapola* and *Green Eyes* and *The Breeze and I* and all those things with Jimmy (Dorsey), with Helen O'Connell, he was the hottest thing...of course, he was one of the nice people in the world." As most of you now know, the Eberly/Eberle's and most other vocalists of the time received only $25.00 per record date. Imagine, that for his terrific recording *Marie Elena,* in my top ten list of the best recordings ever, he received only $25.00. Isn't that hard to believe? But, as Connie Haines told me, that was the deal, and you were growing and being showcased, and so that's all you got. That's one of the reasons why the Society of Singers exists today.

Glenn Miller's vocalist Ray Eberle, 1941. (Richard Grudens Collection)

Ray Eberle sang with Glenn Miller. His quality hits, *Blue Evening, At Last, Serenade in Blue,* and *A Nightingale Sang* in Barkley Square, alone are enough to immortalize him as far as I'm concerned. *That Old Black Magic* and *Elmer's Tune* were pretty good, too! Some say that Glenn never gave Ray enough romantic material to sing compared to what Jimmy Dorsey allowed Bob. Ray was hired by Glenn when Glenn ran into Bob one day and asked," Do you have any brothers who sing like you?" The rest is history. Ray sang for a while with Gene Krupa after leaving Glenn Miller. Most say that Bob had the better voice, but I think I would vote for Ray as an equal. I guess Ray's *Blue Evening* and *Serenade in Blue* influenced my vote. However, thank God for them both. They helped made the Big Band Era more listenable. There is a footnote to this story: Another brother, Walter, was also a singer but never sang with a big name band.

BUDDY CLARK—Oh, Those Doris Day Duets.

Buddy Clark's duets *Love Somebody* and *Baby It's Cold Outside* with Song Star Doris Day are his two most important hits besides his solo rendition of *Linda.*

Born Samuel Goldberg, Buddy started with Gus Arnheim's orchestra, then migrated into Nat Brandwynne's band in the early thirties. He emigrated into Wayne King's band, later becoming a featured vocalist with still another group, Freddy Martin's orchestra. He recorded prolifically with all these groups from 1932 and into the forties. On his one recording with Benny Goodman, Buddy recorded a duet with Helen Ward on a song called *Not Bad.* On a trip back to Hollywood from San Francisco after watching a ball game, he died when the plane crashed. He was thirty-eight. I particularly enjoy his recording *Peg of My Heart,* that illustrates his appealing crooning style. Like Russ Columbo, we'll never know how far he would have gone, if he lived longer.

JOHNNY JOHNSTON—Handsome Is and Handsome Does.

I always liked Johnny Johnston. A vocalist with the Richard Himber band, Johnny is best remembered as an independent soloist, introducing the famous wartime songs *That Old Black Magic, I Don't Want to Walk*

Without You and *Laura.* With Capitol Records he turned out some very good numbers, *Easy to Love, Dearly Beloved,* and *Spring Will Be a Little Late this Year.* He was good looking enough to be selected by Paramount Studios and later MGM for a few movies: *Star Spangled Rhythm, Sweater Girl,* and *You Can't Ration Love* with Paramount and the successful *This Time for Keeps* in 1947 for MGM.

John was a very romantic baritone. In 1951 he appeared in *A Tree Grows in Brooklyn,* a musical, singing *I'll Buy You a Star,* a show stopper if you ever heard one. In those days Johnny would take you aside to proudly show pictures of his little girl Patty Kate, his daughter with actress/singer Kathryn Grayson. If you can find the fairly recent Capitol CD *Great Gentlemen of Song,* you can hear some of Johnny Johnston's best vocals. Johnny passed from us in January 1996 at the age of eighty.

JOHNNY HARTMAN—Mellower Sounds.

Discovering Johnny Hartman is recent for me, thanks to Bob Ramsdell of Madison, Wisconsin. Bob and I regularly talked Hartman through our computers on America Online. He might be Johnny's biggest fan ever.

Born in Chicago, Johnny Hartman sang with the High School glee club and dance band. In his local Baptist church, Johnny had Ruth Jones (Dinah Washington) backing him on piano. "We had so many young people in that church...and our days there were so full of activity. Man, we had a ball." When he entered an amateur contest, he won, and the prize was a week's booking into one of Chicago's large night clubs—which stretched into a year's booking. The acclaim he received convinced him to seek singing as a career.

At seventeen, Johnny performed with Earl Hines for over a year. Then it was time with Dizzy Gillespie, and later recording with John Coltrane, enjoying success in top night clubs across America. "When I'm doing songs from the album I made with Coltrane, I can hear him play...I really can hear him playing the horn," Johnny once said.

In London Johnny worked the Astor Supper Club and stayed for a year on the BBC and other gigs.

"I saw Johnny on two occasions at Ricks, a jazz club in Chicago, the last in February of 1981," Bob Ramsdell told me, "He graciously autographed my Coltrane, *Perception* record album jacket. I also purchased a remarkable album from him that night called *Once In Every Life*. He closed the Coltrane album with a masterful reading of *Lush Life*. His range, dynamics, pitch and diction are without peer." Coltrane rarely recorded with vocalists. Johnny Hartman was Coltrane's unequivocal choice for "the singer I'd like most to be caught with in front of a mike." Born in 1923, Johnny passed away in 1983. He was known as a straightforward highly regarded jazz singer who, when vocalizing, communicated in a rich, smooth baritone in what was originally a Billy Eckstine, Frank Sinatra style.

SAMMY DAVIS, JR.—Will Mastin's Protégé.

I really like Sammy Davis, Jr., but I wasn't around when Harlem first greeted Sammy to life in 1925. His parents were dancers in a black vaudeville troupe known as Will Mastin's Holiday in Dixieland. Sammy was their only child. At age three he made his debut under the name Silent Sam, The Dancing Midget. This old-fashioned hoofer was coached by no less than the master dancer Bill "Bojangles" Robinson, which accounts for Sammy's versatile and dynamic dancing. Sammy was a singer, too. He later paid tribute to Bojangles with his terrific recording of *Mr. Bojangles.*

After serving in the war, Sammy rejoined the group and renamed it the Will Mastin Trio. His inexhaustible energy translated into standing ovations at theater appearances everywhere. Decca signed him in 1954, releasing two albums including *Starring Sammy Davis, Jr.,* which landed in the number one spot. Sammy would do uncanny impressions of all the other men singers. His recording of *Hey There* from *The Pajama Game* was a great success. Then an automobile accident caused him to lose an eye. It is said that Frank Sinatra helped nurse Sammy back to health both physically and emotionally. Upon his return to the stage, Sammy put on an eye-patch and continued to make records and perform. *Something's Gotta Give* and *That Old Black Magic* were two more winners for Sammy, as was *Candyman,* a silly but successful recording, and he scored heavily with his Count Basie Band appearances. Sammy also recorded a number of duets with jazz singer Carmen McRae.

Sammy Davis, Jr. sings in Las Vegas, 1966. (Richard Grudens Collections)

Broadway starred him in *Mr. Wonderful* and ran it for 400 performances, also featuring his uncle and father. The title song and *Too Close for Comfort* were, again, two more winners for Sammy. With Frank Sinatra and others members of Frank's inner circle, Sammy appeared in the films *Ocean's Eleven, Sargeants Three,* and *Robin and the Seven Hoods,* and earlier in *Porgy And Bess,* where he received much acclaim, going on to appear in many other films and Broadway shows including *Golden Boy* in 1964.

Sammy loved—and needed—to sing and proved it going on tour with Frank Sinatra, Dean Martin, and Liza Minelli in the late eighties.

"We had more fun than we deserved," he said. Sammy's book, *Yes, I Can,* is lively reading about an interesting and exciting career. We lost Sammy Davis, Jr. in 1990.

FRED ASTAIRE—He also *sang* the music while he danced.

Last, but never least, Frederick Austerlitz was born in 1899, in Omaha, Nebraska, and became the best non-singer ever, Fred Astaire. In the 1920s and '30s he and his sister Adele worked vaudeville successfully and eventually landed on Broadway. In motion pictures Fred vocally introduced some of the best standards ever written by the pen of Cole Porter, George Gershwin, Irving Berlin, and other composers, in all those Ginger Rogers films and beyond. He introduced *Night and Day, Let's Face the Music and Dance, The Continental, Top Hat, White Tie and Tails,* and *Cheek to Cheek,* to name a few. Not bad, huh! Of course, he also danced a bit now and then. He earned nine Emmy's for just one TV show *An Evening with Fred Astaire* in the early fifties.

Fred Astaire singing *A Fine Romance* in the 1936 film *Swingtime*. (Richard Grudens Collection)

THE ARRANGERS

Musical Architects Writing the Way

Do you recall hearing a favorite singer's or band's newest recording and declaring: "Boy, that was different and unusual—what a great sound!", then thinking, "Wonder who worked out the musical arrangement—who figured out what to play, how to play, and when they should play it"?

The musical arranger, of course!

So, what exactly is an arranger?

"Arranging is the art of adapting a musical composition to a specific instrumental and/or vocal combination. This may range from a single performer, a solo guitar or piano, to a full orchestra with a choir," according to Richard Grudzinski, Associate Professor of Contemporary Writing at Berklee College of Music in Boston. The American Heritage Dictionary defines *arranger* or *arranging* as: "In *Music*. To reset (a composition) for other instruments or voices or for another style of performance."

Professor Grudzinski: "Normally, the arranger works for a client, usually a singer or a band leader for whom he customizes a composition or song. Although the arranger is a vital component to the overall sound (and success) of the artist, they are all too often the unsung heroes of the musical world."

I enjoyed the way legendary arranger Frank De Vol, who arranged Nat Cole's masterpiece *Nature Boy,* illustrated it for me a few days ago while talking to him from his California home: "You get a letter from your mother. You see it and read it, and you actually *see* your mother, not just the words she wrote on paper, but the person you know and love. You picture her perfectly. When I see a melody on a piece of sheet music, I can read it the same way and I can sing it and know what it sounds like without title or words appearing. I know what it sounds like in my mind. Whether it be sad, funny, slow or fast—what it should be, and I can see it clearly. A musician does not have to do that—he just reads the part written for his instrument. An arranger sees and understands all parts and pieces. He takes music and makes it different. He must know how to write for six men, or 17 men, or 100 men, and what will be played and how it will be played, and exactly what it will sound like—much like a painter knows how to create a painting."

Frank DeVol first played lead sax and arranged for popular bandleader Horace Heidt in the 1930's: "Me, Alvino Rey and the four King Sisters were not satisfied with Heidt's material and so we all left to form the Alvino Rey Band where I quit the sax and did all the band's arrangements." In later years, Frank arranged at Columbia Records for Tony Bennett, Doris Day, Peggy Lee, Frankie Laine, and Ella Fitzgerald. He has arranged charts for scores of movies including *Cat Ballou, Guess Who's Coming to Dinner,* and *Hush, Hush, Sweet Charlotte.* Married to Song Star Helen O'Connell for six years before she passed on, Frank is now eighty-two and still working.

Individuality is also affected here, otherwise all bands and singers would wind up sounding pretty much the same. Some classic cases are: Glenn Miller, who worked so long and so hard to find that "special sound" for which he searched so long. When Glenn directed clarinetist Johnny Mince to play the trumpet part with his clarinet when the trumpet player didn't show up for work one night, Glenn's quest ended. By arranging to have the clarinet play on top-playing a double with the tenor below-Glenn Miller's long sought after special intonation finally arrived. Of course, Glenn had arrangers like Bill Finegan and Jerry Gray who were responsible for arranging Glenn's biggest hits. "On the ballads I listen to the words first. That gives me an idea of how to structure the chart," Bill Finegan once said.

Not long ago I remember Kay Starr telling me that George Siravo's very brassy, resounding orchestrations for the stomping sounds of the Charlie Barnet band almost destroyed her vocal chords as she vainly tried to sing above it. Positive for Barnet; trouble for Starr. Kay had to learn to sing all over again because the band's power forced her to sing loudly, ultimately preventing her from singing. "It actually ruined my voice temporarily...it took me over a year to recover." Kay Starr's voice changed after that episode. On the positive side, it was Siravo who wrote the magnificent arrangement of *It's Magic* for Song Star Doris Day, *Who Can I Turn To?* for Tony Bennett, and *When Your Old Wedding Ring Was New* for Jimmy Roselli. He also arranged for Frank Sinatra, Glenn Miller, Gene Krupa, and Charlie Barnet. George Siravo is one of the unsung heroes of the Big Band Era. He and Frank Sinatra worked in tandem for years, and he often "ghosted" for Axel Stordahl at Columbia, turning out some magnificent charts.

Talk about successful arrangements. Tutti Camarata, arranger for Jimmy Dorsey, constricted to three minutes at the end of a radio show, devised a unique formula that featured all the stars of the show. He had boy singer Bob Eberly sing the first chorus of a song as a ballad, then the tempo was to pick up so the entire Dorsey band would play part of the selection, then the tempo was to slow down and Helen O'Connell came in for a semi-wailing finale. We all know the success of *Green Eyes, Amapola,* and *Tangerine*—beautifully arranged by Tutti.

Pete Rugulo, a modernist, progressive, and innovative arranger who studied the careers of Igor Stravinsky (Russian composer of revolutionary musical impact in the modern school) and Darius Milhaud (a French composer who developed polytonality—a simultaneous use of different keys) wrote 90% of Stan Kenton's charts. "In the day when even Benny Goodman and Basie played single harmonies in 4/4 or even 3/4 waltz-time, I added all kinds of dissonants and incorporated some of Milhaud's ideas into jazz using 5/4 material which was never used before," Pete told me just yesterday. He began writing compositions, more like concert pieces, for the Kenton tours. "Stan really liked them—he even had me re-arrange *Artistry in Rhythm,* his great theme." Pete also arranged Billy Strayhorn's *Lush Life* for Nat Cole. "Billy wasn't crazy about the piece. He had it tucked away for ten years. I kind of re-did the verse a lot—I added a lot of bars and stuff. He liked it pretty plain, I think. But I liked it the new way and so did Nat." Pete Rugulo's version is absolutely the most important *Lush Life* ever accomplished on a recording. When speaking to Maria Cole a few weeks ago, she heartily agreed and felt that Pete's arrangement best suited Nat's version of the Strayhorn masterpiece.

Paul Weston arranged and wrote songs (*I Should Care* and *Day by Day*—two Sinatra hits) for five years in the groundbreaking orchestra of Tommy Dorsey. In Hollywood, he arranged the brilliant score for

Bing Crosby and Fred Astaire's terrific Irving Berlin musical film, *Holiday Inn*.

The arranger doesn't just write down notes for musicians to follow, he may actually coach the players and consult closely with the leader of a band. Billy Strayhorn is a fine example. Billy was a composer and arranger for Duke Ellington, who himself was an accomplished orchestrator. But the Duke wanted to expand the band's repertoire, so he hired Strayhorn, who developed into one of the best musical arrangers of the Big Band Era. Billy would utilize the special skills of individual musicians and build the arrangements around their best features, thereby showcasing each player. A great Strayhorn arrangement example was the brilliant *Flamingo* that was recorded by Herb Jeffries. I love that recording.

In discussing the subject with master arranger Billy May, he declares arranging as: "When someone like Irving Berlin writes a song, they usually write just the piano part. If a vocalist is added, they can simply work it out. But, an arranger takes that song and does the background of say an instrumental version, keeping in mind perhaps the addition of a vocalist—figures the key and the vocalists range, and, depending on the mix of instruments you employ, arranges it accord-

Bandleader, arranger Billy May in the 1950's.
(Big Band Jump Collection)

188

ingly. Now, a guy like Sinatra, besides being a great singer, is really a better musician—with fine musical taste—than people give him credit for. He will sit with you for hours and work out what he wants. Does he want to do a ballad with strings, or does he want to work with a dance band sound?"

Billy May is one of the most prolific arrangers of the Age. He has worked with singers like Nat King Cole, who recorded over 60 to 70 sides on *The Billy May Sessions* albums, and on Peggy Lee's album *Pretty Eyes,* as well as Frankie Laine's work at Columbia, on Billy Eckstine's Roulette album, Vic Damone's *Strange Enchantment* album, Ella Fitzgerald's various albums, and Frank Sinatra's recordings. They all owe a lot to his arranging skills. Billy's exceptional introduction to Glenn Miller's *Serenade In Blue* is my favorite.

"With all those singers and bands, it's always a meeting of the minds. You work together to produce the sounds you both want to achieve." Billy began very young playing a tuba in high school, but ended up playing the trumpet: "I became intrigued with the makeup of orchestrations and began making arrangements by the time I was fourteen. I could always tell what the music would sound like in my head. I would utilize the band instruments available in a given band to reach the best effect.

"When I first worked in Hollywood, I would arrange works around the ability of the excellent players who were employed in the established studio bands, so it became easy to get them to accomplish what was needed for a given project." Billy began arranging for Ozzie Nelson's first radio shows; he wrote arrangements for the powerhouse Charlie Barnet band, setting the band's style, and for John Scott Trotter's Orchestra on Bing's famous radio show, including his work with Bing on Decca records. He wrote and played in Glenn Miller's band with fellow arrangers Bill Finegan and Jerry Gray. His own Billy May 1951-53 band wound down (the Big Band Era was over by then) when stationary (no traveling) Hollywood work became available. "I've been here ever since," he said.

I mentioned to Billy that his arrangements of the Time-Life *Big Band Era* albums were my serious introduction to Big Band music. The original 78's, still in the album package, are resting on their laurels on a shelf at home.

An arranger (sometimes working with an instrumentalist) can seize upon a "riff" (a repeated phrase of special character) or catchy phrase, making it a central theme of a given instrumental or vocal. Sometimes arrangers work directly for music publishers, establishing a standard song arrangement for instrument or vocal on a pre-published song sheet.

It's been established over and over again, that when an arranger sets up a chart for a singer by writing his (or her) interpretation of a given composer's work, deciding the combination of instruments that will be used and precisely how those instruments will be played to back up the singer's delivery, the more distinguished the piece. The arranger (who may sometime be a band sideman), usually familiar with the players and singers, as well, capitalizes on his knowledge of their playing abilities.

In the 1930's, Mildred Bailey was once a song-sheet salesgirl in a music shop. She would play the latest song sheets for likely customers. Her interpolated interpretation (arrangement) of a song would help sell the song sheets. When the customer played the selection at home, it usually sounded quite different. As Red Norvo, formerly Mildred's husband and musical director, explained to me, Mildred spontaneously shaded (re-arranged) the piece to suit her voice while demonstrating.

Nat King Cole's recording of the 1946 hit *Nature Boy,* arranged by Nelson Riddle, arguably may not have achieved its melodic greatness without that unique orchestration. Listen carefully to the song's structure as Nat King Cole's voice becomes an instrument playing alongside other instruments. Riddle had converted a simple tune into a rich, uplifting version of what was considered an otherwise dull piece.

One of my earliest friends in this business, the legendary Bill Challis, whose groundbreaking arrangements of Bix Biederbecke's cornet charts and early Bing Crosby vocals with Paul Whiteman's King of Jazz Orchestra have made a difference in how all jazz music of the future was interpreted, was acknowledged by Bing in his autobiography, *Call Me Lucky.* "...Whiteman had progressive arrangers—a fellow named Bill Challis, who arranged vocal licks for us for records and for stage. In that way Al (Rinker) and I kept going and with fresh material." It is believed that Challis was also the first arranger to back instrumental soloists with voices. Challis' work on the song *I'm Comin' Virginia* and

Dardenella were the catalysts for a long-standing jazz style. Bill and I spent many an afternoon at a Long Island bowling alley coffee shop near where he worked, talking about his association with the big bands. In the 1920's orchestra of Jean Goldkette, Bill introduced the "screaming jazz" and peppy gaiety of the Charleston sounds and "whispering cymbals." His use of counter-melody in ensemble, in a way that was used by future bands of the '30s and '40s, revolutionized popular music, the influence so far-reaching that it defies interpretation since its branches and spin-offs are so fragmented now to be almost impossible to trace. Its roots are firmly and recognizably planted deep into the music we know today. The last time I saw Bill was at his Massapequa, Long Island, home sitting in his meticulous garden where he thrived in another kind of harmony, the one with Mother Nature.

Whiteman also employed arrangers Ferde Grofe' (composer of *The Grand Canyon Suite*), who arranged the very first commercial version of George Gershwin's *Rhapsody in Blue,* introduced to the world by Whiteman, and Lennie Hayton (who later worked as musical director at MGM and married Song Star Lena Horne), who wrote many ground-breaking Whiteman charts. Before that, arrangers Fletcher Henderson and Don Redman persevered as special stylists of the emerging black jazz orchestras of the 1930's.

Frank Sinatra is well-known for carefully choosing arrangers to suit a particular style at different times in his career. Sinatra demanded the use of quality arrangers who would enhance his ever-changing style. Upon leaving Tommy Dorsey, Frank selected Axel Stordahl, who expanded Sinatra's vocal repertoire, converting him from a band singer, who sang mostly for dancing, to a gutsy solo performer. Later, when Sinatra joined Capitol Records, Gordon Jenkins, Billy May, and Nelson Riddle worked with him to create a new swinging style that moved Sinatra along and set up his career for even more advances. Professor Richard Grudzinski: "Nelson Riddle created wonderful 'settings' for Frank Sinatra's vocal styling. Nelson knew exactly how to set Sinatra's voice into the picture so as to enhance the performance for the public's enjoyment."

Some arrangers were employed in the bands, and some were hired for specific projects. Fletcher Henderson was hired by Benny Goodman; whereas free-lancer, creative Eddie Sauter, "ten years ahead of his

191

time," according to Glenn Miller, arranged for many bands, including some very special work with the early jazz ensembles of jazz vibraphonist Red Norvo.

"Neal Hefti created great arrangements for the Count Basie Band," Professor Grudzinski explained, "exploiting the band's potential for playing with an incredible 'swing' feel. Neal's Basie chart, *Lil Darlin'*, is a dramatic example of how a band could play with the sense of 'time' and subtlety they possessed."

Here's what author George T. Simon wrote : "Arranging music is a difficult task. It requires a knowledge not only of the basic elements of music but also of form and of exactly what notes each instrument can play and of how they can be most effectively voiced to produce the desired musical effects." Of course, although all arrangers know this, those with the most imagination and skill wind up creating the most original material—the most listenable effect of great arrangements—and thereby occasionally producing a masterpiece.

Many arrangers came out of the big bands: Nelson Riddle first played trombone and arranged for Charlie Spivak; Gordon Jenkins wrote for Isham Jones; Bing Crosby's favorite arranger, John Scott Trotter, first worked for Hal Kemp; Henry Mancini of *Moon River* fame was Tex Beneke's musical writer; Pete Rugolo emanated from Stan Kenton; Edgar Sampson—also a composer (*Don't Be That Way* and *Stompin' at the Savoy*) wrote for Chick Webb; Neal Hefti worked for Basie and, with Ralph Burns, played and arranged for Woody Herman (Woody once told me he never arranged, but that he was a good editor). Axel Stordahl, Paul Weston, and Sy Oliver all were established Tommy Dorsey arrangers who went on to arrange for many future bands and singers, and Bobby Haggart wrote arrangements for the Bob Crosby Band with the help of Matty Matlock and Deane Kincaide. Bob Crosby called Haggart "the undiscovered George Gershwin of our day." Bob is the author of the song *What's New?* among others. And, as noted, Frank De Vol began his arranging career with Horace Heidt.

The bandleaders appreciated the arrangers: "Fletcher. He was *the* arranger," said ace drummer and band leader Gene Krupa, "and my first band back in the thirties was the best I ever had—with Fletcher Henderson." "Fletcher was one of the great orchestrators of the era," Benny

Goodman told me back in 1984, "his arrangements were fascinating—you always hear something different each time you hear a number,"

Mel Tormé, an arranger himself, said: "My early role models cling to me with a kind of musical static electricity: Fletcher and (Eddie) Sauter, Jerry Gray. Duke himself. And the latter-day saints: Jerry Mulligan and Gil Evans, Marty Paich, Neal Hefti and Ralph Burns, and so many more."

"While I was at Columbia (Records)," said my friend Frankie Laine, whose appreciation of quality arranging is evident in his work, "I had the chance to work with some of the greatest arranging talents in the business: Paul Weston, Percy Faith, Frank DeVol and others, who helped build my career through their great arrangements."

Arrangements are extremely important to a song. Take Cole Porter's masterpiece *Begin the Beguine*. "...when you're Cole Porter and you write *Begin the Beguine* and it drops dead, and suddenly a guy named Artie Shaw comes along and makes a record of it with a totally different arrangement from what you wrote, and that becomes a hit," bandleader Artie Shaw told my colleague, writer Fred Hall, for his book *Dialogues in Swing* in 1989. The Shaw arrangement is the definitive recording of that great standard. The arranger was Jerry Gray.

Arrangers and their arrangements *are* everything in music. Ask any musician, ask any singer.

THE EUROPEANS
The Music Men Over There

MAX WIRZ: It's Showtime

How does a chapter about the work of a Swiss Big Band disc jockey find its way into an American book about American singers, arrangers, and composers?

It's easy!

Just call Frankie Laine.

Frankie Laine, who needs no introduction to most Americans or Europeans, is the kind of a guy you wish you had as a friend all your life. Fortunately for me, our association began backstage at Westbury Music Fair in the mid-eighties while interviewing him for Long Island PM Magazette. Since then, we have maintained a close relationship, mostly by phone and mail—always conversing about our kind of music, and the players and singers.

Now, it seems that Frank had the same effect on another interviewer, Max Wirz, who conducts a *Make Believe Ballroom* kind of radio show on FM Radio Thurgau, in the pretty Swiss town of Frauenfeld, near Lake Constance. Max calls his show *Light and Breezy*. His heroes are the same as yours and mine: Perry Como, Bing Crosby, Ray Anthony, Les and Larry Elgart, Frankie Laine, Frank Sinatra, Rosemary Clooney, Doris Day and all the other song stars we love so well. Max regularly sends me cassettes of his shows.

It was not until December 1985, when Switzerland opened its airwaves to privately owned radio stations, that Max found the fulfillment of a dream he had carried secretly with him ever since he heard those first American Forces Network (AFN) broadcasts and since he saw those B movies with Gene Autry, Roy Rogers and the Sons of the Pioneers. Max widely criticized the terrible noises when he heard the first broadcast on the new station and complained to the station manager who suggested: "If you are so smart, why don't you come down to the station and do it yourself."

Three weeks later, easy-going Max Wirz, now a sixty-four year old Swiss-US dual citizen, was on the air with a two-hour program first entitled *It's Showtime,* with music from films, Broadway, and beautiful Big Band sounds, which we label our kind of music. From 1954, Max lived in the U S for 17 years, served as a sargeant in the New York National Guard, spent two years in the U.S. Army, held jobs with Swissair and E.F. Hutton in New York and Chicago, all while listening to radio station WPAT, Paterson, New Jersey; WAIT, Chicago, and WNEW, New York. Max married his schooldays sweetheart, Nelly, in

My friends Max Wirz (right) of Radio Thurgau in Switzerland and Don Kennedy of Big Band Jump Radio, posing after having been on the air on WQXI, Atlanta, Georgia, broadcasting a special edition of Max's *It's Showtime,* a regular radio program with beautiful big band sounds. October 1992.

1958. In 1970, he returned to Switzerland with Nelly and their 8 year-old son, Tom.

"I owned about 30 to 40 LPs, which Nelly and I bought as far back as the fifties." he said, "I had a concept. I wanted to play lots of music, give the listeners a hint of what I was trying to do with a few remarks, but most of all, play music. After two shows I ran out of material. I browsed through music stores and purchased more." (The inventory today: a private cache of 1,100 CDs, 750 LPs, 200 cassettes, and a completely equipped sound studio to research, edit and produce portions of his shows.)

"*It's Showtime,* my first show, opened with Glenn Millers' version of *In The Mood* and closed two hours later with Harry James' version of *Sleepy Time Gal.* With America's best Broadway musicals, Big Band Sounds, Dixieland, and Western Swing, I bring American history, geography and all holiday traditions to my listeners. There are theme shows for Christmas and New Year's, and all the other holidays including Thanksgiving, complete with Turkey-carving and stuffing instructions."

Over a period of about eleven years, Max and Nelly traveled to America. Five cruises, including two sponsored by *Big Band Jump,* gave Max the opportunity to see more of America while interviewing music greats Ray Anthony, Frankie Laine, Les Elgart, Nancy Knorr, and our mutual friend Don Kennedy, host of *Big Band Jump,* a nationally syndicated Big Band radio program originating from Atlanta, Georgia, also heard on cable overseas."

Upon writing the second book in this series, *The Song Stars,* I asked Frankie Laine if he knew anyone who could furnish first-hand information about expatriate singer Josephine Baker and France's "little sparrow" singer, Edith Piaf. That's when Max Wirz entered my life. Max was able to recommend Andre' Doudot, a friend living in the French part of Switzerland, who actually knew Josephine Baker when he was young. His father and Miss Baker were members of the French Resistance. When Josephine Baker became ill, Andre's family secretly cared for her on their small farm in Morocco, North Africa while she convalesced. The story of Miss Baker is chronicled in *The Song Stars.* Max feels honored and flattered to be included in this book, but it is I who am flattered and honored. Here is his story about the Music Men Over There:

Hazy Osterwald, and Others—Putting On a Show by Max Wirz.

Over the years Switzerland played an important role in the development of jazz and Big Band music on the European continent. Fred Boehler, a Swiss jazz pioneer who passed away at age 83 in 1995, had his story published, the definitive book on the subject, *Swiss Jazzpioneer Fred Boehler: His Life, His Music.* When browsing through music stores in Zurich and other cities, through sparse notes on LP and CD sleeves, one cannot escape the name of Hazy Osterwald, who is America's Ray Anthony, Harry James, Benny Goodman, Louis Prima, and Glenn Miller all rolled into one. For the past 50 years Hazy led a big band, then a Sextet, later renamed the Jetset, and more recently performs with The Entertainers.

Born on February 18, 1922, he is a musician, arranger, composer, and band leader, another early prophet of jazz. Today, Hazy is one of the still active personalities who lived through the development of musical entertainment from the thirties up to the present. Hazy and I sat down to talk about his life and career on December 29, 1997 at his apartment in the Grand Hotel National, Lucerne, Switzerland.

"You ask me the secret of my success, Max. Well I always try to select the best musicians, arrangers, choreographers, and roadies. I look

Veteran Swiss disc jockey Max Wirz (right) with Hazy Osterwald.

197

for music that catches the audience. I try to do it right, give it the best I have to give, never worry about cost (he smiles) because if you're successful, you can pay the price for the best. Most of all though, we did not just play music, we did what Americans do, **we put on a show."**

Originally, young Hazy was interested in playing soccer (his mother canceled his piano lessons for lack of interest), but, in 1938, when he heard a small college band playing that "new American sound" called *jazz,* he changed his mind forever. He took those piano lessons again and won acceptance in a band playing *September in the Rain,* but took up the horn (he calls it Susie after a late 1940s fable about a Vienna Symphonic Orchestra male trombone and female tuba who fell in love and *Susie* the trumpet was born) to become a front man and eventually a band leader. "It was a smaller world then. We did not have entertainment as we understand it today," he said. "In the countryside there were folklore groups, yodeling and playing their kind of music at county fairs. In cities like Zurich, Bern, and Geneva, there were orchestras playing in hotels and clubs, and smaller groups for afternoon teas and for after dinner dancing."

There were not any Big Bands around then: "Remember, this was the time when Adolf Hitler built the Reich. That kind of music was forbidden in German occupied territory all around Switzerland, and not heard on radio or in films. That made it difficult for American jazz to get a foothold." As youngsters, they were happy to catch Ernest Berner playing jazz on his piano, or listen to records that found their way into Switzerland one way or another.

"I remember some of the symphonic jazz and straight dance music played by Paul Whiteman and Englishman Jack Hylton," Hazy recalled. For most, real jazz was rare.

During the thirties, Teddy Stauffer, a Swiss saxophone player made his way through Germany with a 10 to 16 piece show orchestra. It was called Teddy Stauffer and his Original Teddies and performed at the 1939 Swiss Fair.

"Fred Boehler, a piano player, an early jazz musician, and pioneer at the organ performed in the Fashion Pavilion there with a six-piece orchestra," Hazy went on to say, "When World War II broke out, Switzerland became isolated. Some musicians returned to their own countries. Teddy Stauffer went to Canada, then to Acapulco where he became a hotel man. Ernst Hoellerhagen, the Benny Goodman of Europe, took over the Teddies. Fred Boehler expanded to a full band and in 1941 took me on as second trumpet and part time arranger."

The band played *The St. Louis Blues, Back Home In Indiana,* and all the music played by the Big Bands of America. They tried to present it like the Americans did, with a little bit of showmanship. As the war moved on, most band members saw Swiss military service and played only occasionally. "It was rough to be a professional musician," Hazy said, "I joined the Teddies in 1943 and we did *Deep In the Heart of Texas, Goody Goody,* and the *Pagan Love Song.* The music was good, but it was a difficult time. Fred's band, The Teddies, and Bob Engel's Big Band in Geneva were lucky to play a few one-nighters and an occasional half-hour concert on Swiss National Radio."

Hazy's trumpet-playing idol was Louis Armstrong, and then came Harry James. "I liked Harry's more progressive sound and began to work on it." In 1944, Hazy had his world premiere at the then famous Chikito Club in Bern as leader of the Hazy Osterwald Orchestra, an eight-piece group with singer Kitty Ramon. "We did James' *Two O'Clock Jump,* Count Basie's *Jumpin'at the Woodside,* Glenn's *In the Mood,* Kitty sang Tommy Dorsey's *I'm Getting Sentimental Over You,* a couple of us teamed up with Kitty for *Chattanooga Choo Choo.* Then we did Benny's *Swing Time in the Rockies.*"

In 1948 the band toured Europe with 16 pieces, but could not get enough work. "So I slimmed down to six men. On May 1, 1949, the Hazy Osterwald Sextet, with Ernst Hoellerhagen, Pierre Cavalli, Gil Cuppini, Sunny Lang, Francis Burger, and I, opened at the Salle Pleyel in Paris during the Paris Jazz-Festival."

In 1950, now a well-known, the London magazine *Melody Maker* wrote, "It takes a Swiss band to show us!" In 1952 they landed a six months contract to play in America at the Beverly Hills Hotel. Unfortunately, the U.S. musicians union torpedoed the deal. From 1952 through '55, the group signed up for USO shows from North Africa to Scotland. When not entertaining at U.S. Army, Navy and Air Force bases, they toured throughout Europe and Russia, they appeared in films, on television and records, and in famous clubs, resorts, and theaters.

"We did it American style," Hazy explained, "appearing with the best of Europe's entertainers, including Big Band men Kurt Edelhagen,

Paul Kuhn, Horst Jankowski, Max Greger, and singers Lys Assia, Caterina Valente', and the Kessler Twins. In 1964 and 1976 the sextet was the official Olympic Orchestra during the Winter Olympics in Innsbruck, Austria." In 1972, they also performed in Munich.

In 1970 they were allowed to tour the USA as the Hazy Osterwald Jetset. During the '70s they played in Aspen and Vail, Colorado, and did some club dates in Chicago where they appeared on television. When I wondered if they ever had any million sellers, Hazy replied, "I never hit gold. It took a million sales within a given period of time. The *Kriminal-Tango,* an unusual German song, was one that surpassed the million mark long ago. Over the years we successfully produced 35 LPs and 125 singles, and we are still at it."

It was not always easy traveling the globe with his group. Just like their American counterparts, the group ran into surprises like having differences of opinion with club owners and record companies, not to mention the unfortunate flat tires on the road and the snow storms without tire-chains. "But, our audiences and we had a good time."

Today, Hazy Osterwald, musician and showman, maintains and keeps developing his jazz repertoire. He plays vibraphone with The Swing Makers and with The Willy Bischof Jazztet, and still has fun with his group Hazy Osterwald and The Entertainers, a nine-piece show band. "It is gratifying to play to smaller audiences who appreciate the kind of jazz which we took over from our American idols."

On December 20, 1997, during a two-hour special on Swiss

European Legend Hazy Osterwald celebrates a lifetime of music. (Max Wirz photo)

TV, Hazy Osterwald was honored with a Lifetime Achievement Award. At the same time, Hans Zurbruegg, manager of the International Jazz Festival at Bern, presented him with the Three Keys Award, an honor earlier bestowed on such jazz greats as Stephane Grappelli and Oscar Peterson. The Mayor of the City of Bern declared him to be an Ambassador of the City of Bern. Hazy has performed over 100,000 hours before audiences and cameras and has traveled 5,000,000 miles performing around the globe. We know that many an American GI saw Hazy perform in those USO shows, and many a ski fan in the Rockies and visitors to European cities, where he and his music could be enjoyed, also remember and recognize Hazy Osterwald as a true Music Man Over There.

Looking into the development of jazz and Big Bands in Switzerland, we must take note of Ernest R. Berner and his son Andre'"Andy" Berner. Ernest is a true jazz pioneer. In the twenties he lived in Paris where he followed the jazz scene. He once substituted as a piano player in Paul Whiteman's great *King of Jazz* Orchestra, played with Coleman Hawkins for two years, and became a sought-after accompaniest for working jazz greats like Louis Armstrong, whom Ernest contracted for his first concert in Switzerland in 1934. I talked with Ernest's son, semi-retired Andy Berner, in his office, high above the Bellevue Platz in Zurich, and learned a few things about him.

"I also took piano lessons, but, my father thought my progress was too slow, so I switched to drums, which I enjoyed more, and played with many combos and small bands right into the fifties," Andy told me, "Although I graduated in architecture, through my father and my own musical ambitions, I was drawn into the jazz world. In 1951, I organized the first Jazz Festival in Zurich, and, by spending all my spare time and much of my own money, continued to do so right into the seventies. We gave amateur jazz bands of Switzerland a chance to perform before large, attentive audiences." In later years they added amateur bands from abroad, and famous names to give exhibition concerts. Practically all the big names in jazz of the sixties and seventies thrilled our audiences." Andy said.

Wondering if Andy was involved with any such events today, he explained: "Not with big ones. However, I have been connected lately with Jazz in Zollikon, in the suburb of Zurich, presenting jazz combos

201

and Big Bands. Musicians like Pepe Lienhard, who runs the Big Band of the Swiss Army, Hazy Osterwald (known as Mr. Swiss Jazz), the living legend, Willy Schmid of the Smeed Trio, Willy Bischof, jazz piano, and George Gruntz, Switzerland's foremost jazz professor, act as festival jury." The Max Gerlach Big Band, Pat's Big Band, and other volunteers spend hours practicing and performing with no more reward than a standing ovation and a 'Bratwurst und es Glas Bier."

That's it, Richard, and dear readers. Thanks that I could contribute the part of the story of Europe's, and particularly Switzerland's Big Band scene to all of you. Keep swinging and smiling, America.

Frank Touhey of Montpellier Records, Cheltenham, England and Max Wirz (right) choosing one of Ray Anthony's songs for Light and Breezy on Radio Thurgau. (Richard Grudens Collection)

THE BIG BAND HALL OF FAME

Sally Bennett's Quest Comes True

Back in Cleveland, in the 1960's, and even earlier in Atlanta, Georgia, when Sally Bennett featured composers, musicians, and vocalists on her radio and television"talk show" which included most of the nation's top Big Band leaders and vocalists, she conceived the idea of instituting a Big Band Hall of Fame to honor the great individuals who graced the bandstands and brought the music we have all come to cherish during the Big Band Era and beyond.

Big Band Hall of Fame President Sally Bennett with Harry James and his long time manager PeeWee Monte in 1971. (Sally Bennett Collection)

Sally, with the help of her businessman husband Paul, began collecting some unique items, now held in storage in Miami : Billy Butterfield's and Harry James' trumpet; Glenn Miller's and Sammy Kaye's bandstand jackets; the mirrored ball from Chicago's famous Aragon Ballroom, Russ Morgan's trombone, and various pieces of music, bandstand objects, books, and memorabilia. All these objects will be part of a Big Band Museum now under design and renovation in a West Palm Beach, Florida, building located at 813 Gardenia Street, once the Mediterranean Revival Building of Palm Beach Junior College from 1933 to 1948.

The purpose of the museum is to commemorate the famous Big Bands and their all-American, prestigious popular music. As the idea evolved, musicians and other interested individuals joined up, contributing further reminders of the Big Band Era.

Lot's of folks you know are on the Hall of Fame Honorary Board, including Perry Como, Al Ham, Burt Reynolds, Donald Trump, Merv Griffin, Joni James, and our friend, Bob Hope. Not a bad roster of supporters, you will agree. Last year, Music Man Don Cornell was inducted into the Big Band Hall of Fame. This year, Song Star Dolly Dawn will be inducted during a charity ball at Donald Trump's Mar-a-Largo estate.

Talking to Sally one evening in late January, 1998, she urged me to ask you readers to write her, perhaps send a piece of cherished memorabilia to her for use in the museum in order to give future generations a glimpse of what life was like during the Big Band Era.

Sally Bennett, President and Founder
BIG BAND HALL OF FAME
Sutton Place South—# 305
2778 South Ocean Boulevard
Palm Beach, Florida 33480

AL HAM—Much Music of Your Life.

You could travel from city to city throughout the United States and you would be accompanied by radio station after radio station playing, well, the music of your life. The *Music of Your Life* is exactly that: All the bands, all the singers in those bands, and all the singers and musicians who immediately followed the Big Band Era. Certainly, all the subjects in this book and my previous books, *The Song Stars* and *The Best Damn Trumpet Player,* as well as George Simon's chronicle, *The Big Bands,* and Will Friedwald's definitive book on singers and musicians, *Jazz Singing,* will perform for you on the faithful AM dial.

Music of Your Life is actually a syndicated radio format first created and managed by musician, composer, and arranger Al Ham in 1977 on radio station WDJC in Bridgeport, Connecticut. Al played bass for Artie Shaw when he was merely seventeen. He arranged music for Tony Pastor's band while Rosemary and Betty Clooney were the band's singers. When Tex Beneke re-formed the Glenn Miller Orchestra after World War II, Al sat in with his bass. Later, Henry Mancini hired Al Ham as an arranger.

Al Ham's recording credits include a number of Columbia best-selling evergreens: the original cast albums *My Fair Lady, West Side Story, Most Happy Fella,* and *Gypsy,* among others. While with Columbia, Al produced an unknown Johnny Mathis recording entitled *Wonderful, Wonderful,* the song that catapulted Johnny into fame and fortune. "When I first heard it on the radio, one year after it was first recorded, I knew I would be a singer for all my life. I was in awe, believe me," Johnny told me just recently, "and I still am."

Al's unique singing group, *The Hillside Singers,* recorded the tremendous hit *I'd Like To Teach the World to Sing.* He arranged and produced that gem, too. Al has composed and arranged many commercials for radio and has even received an Academy Award Nomination for an adaptation and scoring of the Warner Brothers film *Stop the World—I Want To Get Off.* He also received a Grammy for his production of James Whitmore's *Give 'Em Hell Harry.*

Afraid America was losing the music exposure battle to rock & roll, Al Ham rallied to the cause by introducing his *Music of Your Life* formula to radio stations throughout the country. He may well have saved "our kind of music" through this remarkable radio vehicle, even spawning imitators by causing other radio stations of the genre' to re-shape their format to the magical *Music of Your Life* formula. It kept performers like Johnny Mathis, Tony Bennett, Frank Sinatra, Frankie Laine, Ella Fitzgerald, Peggy Lee, Bing Crosby, and others consistently on the air everyday, everywhere. His salesmanship and ideas, through his knowledge of all phases of the music business, kept these and other performers in the recording studio and permitted listeners to tune in to the music they love best, the *Music of Your Life,* my life, and Al's life where Bing Crosby will sing for you, Ray Anthony will play for you, and the Mills Brothers will harmonize for you.

Stay tuned.

An excellent singer in her own right, Ann Jillian talks Music Men to Richard Grudens, backstage during *Sugar Babies* performance. (photo–C. Camille Smith)

HONORABLE MENTIONS

More Unforgettable Vocalists

**Richard Grudens with singer Earl Wrightson and singer
Lois Hunt in Brookville, Long Island in the early eighties.
(photo by Gus Young)**

Andy Russell, the ultimate gentleman singer, began in Gus Arnheim's band where both **Bing** and **Russ Columbo** developed their vocals. Andy sang with the Mitchell Ayres Orchestra on his own TV show during 1944 &'45. The classics *Besame Mucho* and *What a Difference a Day Makes* mark him as a world-class singer. I always loved his thrilling version of *Amor* and *Laughing on the Outside*. Born Andres Rubago Perez in the Mexican section of East L.A. in 1919, Andy epitomized Chicano music and became a favorite during the '50s and '60s in Latin America and Cuba where he continually toured. Andy and I once sat down together in the '80s at radio station WLIM on Long Island.

Composer, singer, arranger **Matt Dennis** began in vaudeville and was engaged by Tommy Dorsey as a writer for **Frank Sinatra's,** Jo Stafford's, and Connie Haines' special material. He worked with the Glenn Miller Army Air Force band, acted on TV, sang and played piano and sang in nightclubs. *Let's Get Away from It All* and *The Night We Called it a Day* were two of his songs. His song *Angel Eyes* was performed in the film *Jennifer* in 1953.

Bill Kenny, Orville "Happy" Jones, Charlie Fuqua, and **Ivory "Deek" Watson** were the original **Ink Spots,** one of the best singing quartets ever. Throughout the forties they produced numbers like *We*

The incomparable Bill Kenny and the Ink Spots.
(Richard Grudens Collection)

Three, I Don't Want to Set the World On Fire, I'm Making Believe, and, with Ella, *Cow-Cow-Boogie* and *Into Each Life Some Rain Must Fall.* I liked the **Ink Spots** doing *If I Didn't Care*—didn't you? **Al Rivers,** a later **Ink Spot** from 1949 to 1958, recorded all the famous numbers and even started another **Ink Spot** group in 1985.

Al Hibbler was *the* blues singer for Duke Ellington for eight years. "He had so many sounds that even without words he could tell of fantasy beyond fantasy," said Duke in his book *Music is My Mistress.* Although he was blind like **Ray Charles, Frank Sinatra** called them both "my two ace pilots." **Hibbler's** *After the Lights Go Down Low* is a classic and is filled with the famous **Hibbler** sounds as is his rendition of *Unchained Melody.*

Arthur Prysock, an **Eckstine** follower, sang robust rhythm and blues and some standards. His voice was commanding. **Arthur** became famous singing in Buddy Johnson's band after World War II. He developed into a romantic ballad vocalist during the 1950's doing mostly club dates. **Prysock's** voice was always rich and lush. Might mention that **Glen Douglas** was a **Prysock-Eckstine** style singer for Tex Beneke's big band.

Old Rocking Chair **singer and composer Hoagy Carmichael
(Richard Grudens Collection)**

Hoagy Carmichael, best known as the writer of the immortal *Stardust,* often performed his own songs on records like *Rockin' Chair, Up a Lazy River, Two Sleepy People* and *Ole Buttermilk Sky,* among his best.

Thomas Traynor, singer, writer and arranger, started with the Bob Mitchell Boys Choir in 1935 and eventually toured with Jan Garber's, Frankie Masters', Benny Goodman's, and Jerry Gray's bands. He joined Glenn's Modernaires vocal group and stayed until 1992. **Don Reid** sang on the bandstand with Sammy Kaye, Xavier Cugat, and Henry King. He also penned *Remember Pearl Harbor,* a blockbuster wartime hit, and wrote music for **Eddie Fisher** and Patti Page, winning both an Emmy and Peabody award for his TV manuscripts.

Smith Ballew conducted and carried the vocals in his own band beginning in the 1920's after some time with Leo Reisman. He could handle any lyric. Later, he sang with Ben Pollack, Ted Fio Rito, and Hal Kemp. He re-formed his band again in 1929, becoming the singing host on radio's *Shell Chateau* program. **Russ Carlyle, Tommy Ryan,** and **Clyde Burke** all chirped with **Blue Barron,** whose late '40s hit *Cruising Down the River* hit the top of the charts. **Blue** also sang with Russ Carlyle's band a little bit earlier. **Tony Barron** also sang with his own band in the 1960's. His song *How I Miss You When the Summer is Gone,* was also his theme. **Earl Warren** was a singer with Count Basie, but not as well-known as most Basie vocalists. **Greg Lawrence** sang alongside Eydie Gorme' in **Tex Beneke's** post-war band as well as in Frankie Carle's. **Bunny Berigan** sang in his own band, especially the number one Big Band Era hit *I Can't Get Started,* which was also his theme. **Chick Bullock** and **Art Gentry** also vocalized with **Berigan, Gentry** later working with Nat Brandwynne.

Frank Bettencourt fronted and sang his theme *Dreams of You* in his own band in the 1960's. Canadian vocalist **Dick Todd** was also a shining star. A husky voice, developed while a trumpet player, was his trademark. In 1938 he recorded for Bluebird and was featured in New York at the Strand Theater. **Dick** was known as the Canadian **Bing Crosby.** His 1949 hit, *Daddy's Little Girl,* and his recording of *Blue Orchids* were superior efforts. Drummer **Ray McKinley** (who later formed his own band) vocalized in Will Bradley's, warbling a lot of boogie-woogie material like *Beat Me Daddy Eight to the Bar* and later

You Came A Long Way from St.Louis. **Tiny Bradshaw** handled the vocals in his own band in the 1930's and recorded on Decca as did **Chuck Cabot.**

Ray Kellogg sang with Les Brown's Band of Renown, as did **Ralph Young** and **Butch Stone,** who performed comedy numbers and is still with Les to this day. Known as either the **Four Recorders** or the **Three Strikes, Carl Grayson, Bob Hannon, Skip Morr, Tom Huston, Dick Wharton,** and **Billy Sherman** all dished up the vocals with Henry Busse in the 1930's in Cinncinati. Bob Chester's vocalists were **Al Stuart, Bill Darnell, Bill Reynolds,** and **Gene Howard—The Rhythmaires. Gene** also sang with Stan Kenton, sharing the bill with Anita O'Day. **Ford Leary** helped bandleader Larry Clinton with some vocals.

Can't help but note the career of my friend and fellow Long Islander **Earl Wrightson.** He was hardly a band singer but he sang our kind of music on *The Coca Cola Hour* and hosted a 15-minute show called *At Home.* He starred in *Can Can, Kiss Me Kate,* and *Man of La Mancha* on Broadway. **Gary Crosby** deserves a mention too. He dueted with dad **Bing** on records backed by the big band of John Scott Trotter and others. Remember *Sam's Song* and *Play a Simple Melody?* Gary wrote a sour book about his dad which he later recanted. He passed away of lung cancer in 1995 at 62.

Jim Blair, now a Big Band disc jockey in Titusville, Florida, sang with Teddy Powell, Guy Lombardo, Eddie Duchin, and Lawrence Welk. They call him "Mr. Big Band" down Florida way.

Bobby Darin had much to be appreciated. He could switch from a **Hank Williams** twang to a **Ray Charles** genius, at the drop of a hat, especially on the song *I Got a Woman.* Born in Harlem, New York, **Bobby** always was a swinging kid. Everyone knows his version of *Mack the Knife* is *the* definitive.

The Coon-Sanders Kansas City Nighthawks vocals were delivered by **Carleton Coon** and **Joe Sanders,** themselves beginning in early 1919 with their hit *Hi Diddle Diddle,* mostly at the Blackhawk Restaurant. **Kenny Sargent's** strong vocals with Francis Craig included *Red Rose* and *Near You.* **Bing's** brother, **Bob Crosby,** performed both chores for his own band, previously singing with Anson Weeks and the Dorsey Brothers. **Frank Munn** worked the Bernie Cummins band in Indiana at the Toadstool Inn (and with Leo Reisman, then Eddy Duchin a little later), as did **Jerry Lang. Phil Brito** did the honors with Al Donahue along with **Snooky Lanson,** the guy who eventually sang all those hits on *The Hit Parade* television show with Song Star Dorothy Collins. **Snooky** also performed with Ray Noble at Catalina Island,California.

John Gary's first album *Catch a Rising Star* earned him a long-time contract with RCA in the '60s, and a Grammy nomination in 1963 as best new artist. His cherubic countenance and his voice of "magic" has endured throughout the years. He is the total entertainer with over 28 albums. I like his *John Gary Sings Cole Porter* album on which he excels. He should have been greater. We lost John in January 1998.

The Dorseys, Jimmy and Tommy, had lots of boy singers. Besides **Frank Sinatra** and **Dick Haymes,** Tommy employed spiffy **Jack Leonard** (Remember *Marie?*) and **Stuart Foster** (who also sang with Ina Ray Hutton). Besides featuring **Bob Eberly,** Jimmy also presented **Phil Washburn** as the boy singer. Among Eddy Duchin's vocalists were **Jimmy Newell, Buddy Clark,** and **Tony Leonard, Sonny Washburn** was the boy singer for Shep Fields. Jack Fina featured **Harry Prime** (also with Ralph Flanagan's band) and **Gil Lewis. Muzzy Marcellino** warbled along with **Stanley Hickman** in the Ted Fio Rita band and later in his own band in 1938. **Jimmy Castle** singing *Oh, You Beautiful Doll* toured with Chuck Foster's band in the late thirties.

Harry Barris was one of the vocalists with **Bing** and **Al Rinker** in the original **Rhythm Boys** singing with Paul Whiteman and his King of Jazz Orchestra. He helped write *Mississippi Mud, I Surrender, Dear* (with Bing) and *Wrap Your Troubles in Dreams.* After Whiteman, he became a solo entertainer.

Jan Garber featured a bunch of male singers over the years: **Lee Bennett, Tony Allen, Tim Reardon, Alan Copeland** (also sang with Jerry Gray's band), **Bob Grabeau, Roy Cordell, Larry Dean,** and **Marv Nielsen. Art Lund** recorded one of the era's best loved hits, *Mamselle',* but not with Benny Goodman for whom he also sang. **Art Berry** and **Johnny Victor** exercised their lungs with Gray Gordon in the early 1960's. **Pee Wee Hunt** (who also doubled on the trombone), and **Jack Richman** were boy singers for Glen Gray's Casa Loma Orchestra.

Before our own Dolly Dawn took over George Hall's band, he featured **Irving Kaufman** and **Barry Wells** on the vocals. Before Dorsey, original Pied Piper **Clark Yocum** first sang with Mal Hallett. Before jazz pianist Lennie Hayton joined MGM, he featured **Paul Barry** on the vocals in his own band. Horace Heidt had a bunch of boy singers too: **Larry Cotton; Charles Goodwin; Red Farrington; Art Carney** (yes, **Art Carney,** the Norton of *The Honeymooners*); Gordon McRae (Yes, the one of *Oklahoma & Carousel* fame); **Frank De Vol** (Helen O'Connell's husband, bandleader and arranger); and **Ronnie Kemper.**

Ray Herbecks' Los Angeles band included **Hal Munbar, Kirby Brooks** and **Ray Olsen** as boy singers. **Woody Herman** had lots of girl singers, but only he handled the boy singer chores. Remember *Caldonia?* I knew and loved **Woody Herman.** Big **Tiny Hill** also did some of his own vocals, but with some help from **Al deWitt, Al Larsen,** and **Bob Freeman.** Besides **Johnny Mercer, Guy Russell, Joey Nash** and **Stuart Allen** sang with Richard Himber's band. **Arthur Lee Simpkins** was also one of Earl Fatha Hines' vocalists. **Buddy De Vito,** guitarist **Buddy Moreno** (who later sang in his own band), and **Ernie Andrews** all were once Harry James' boy singers. **Buddy** sounded so much like **Frank Sinatra** on so many sides.

Art Jarrett handled his own band vocals at the Blackhawk in Chicago in the thirties. Spike Jones spawned singers **George Rock** and **Red Ingall** in his crazy band. **Bill Darnell** sang with Al Kavelin. **Marty McKenna, Clyde Burke, Arthur Wright,** and **Tommy Ryan** handled some of Sammy Kaye's vocals.

Bob Allen and **Scrappy Lambert** were featured with Hal Kemp, **Gene Howard** and **Jay Johnson** with Stan Kenton. Bandleader Henry King hired **Dick Robertson** (also with Leo Reisman later-on), **Ray Hunkel, Don Reid, Sidney Sudy, Sonny Schuyler, Don Raymond,** and **Phil Hanna** for his guy vocalists in the early thirties. Besides whistling for his supper, **Elmo Tanner** (Remember *Heartaches?*) sang for Wayne King with fellow vocalist **Charles Farrell.** Drummer favorite Gene Krupa employed **Howard Dulany,** the exceptional voice of **Johnny Desmond, Buddy Hughes, Dave Lambert** (later became part of **Lambert, Hendricks,** and **Ross** ace singing group), and **Buddy Stewart** as boy singers.

Kay Kyser's popular band featured **Merwyn Bogue** (known to all as the silly-singing **Ishkabibble**), **Bill Stoker,** the personable **Harry Babbitt,** and **Mike Douglas** (Yes, Mike Douglas of TV fame) as his guy singers. Guy Lombardo's brother-in-law **Kenny Gardner** handled the band's sweet vocals, as did brother **Carmen Lombardo.** Johnny Long supported vocalists **Paul Harman** and **Bob Houston.** Vincent Lopez spawned a batch of male vocalists: **Jack Parker, Frank Munn, Johnny Morris,** and **Sonny Schuyler.** Great arranger **Sy Oliver** once sang with Jimmie Lunceford's band, as did **Dan Grissom, Joe Thomas, Henry Wells,** and trombonist **Trummy Young.** NBC's 1950's producer **Barry Wood** once sang with Abe Lyman.

Freddie Stewart and **Wayne Gregg** were singers with Clyde McCoy of *Sugar Blues* fame and Hal McIntyre had **Carl Denny** on his bandstand. Ralph Marterie hired **Bill Walters** and **Lou Prano** to do the vocals. Freddy Martin's best singer was enterpreneur and TV host **Merv Griffin** (Remember *I've Got a Lovely Bunch of Coconuts?*). **Russ Morgan** (later a bandleader himself), **Eddie Stone, Clyde Rogers, Bill Stoker, Johnny Cochran,** and **Marty Barris** were also Martin vocalists. Frankie Masters had **Harlan Rogers, Gordon Goodman,** and **Lou Hurst** on the bandstand. **Skip Nelson** sang some great numbers with Glenn Miller.

Besides himself, **Vaughn Monroe** featured **Johnny Turnbull,** with novelty numbers performed by sideman **Ziggy Talent. Russ Morgan** did most of his own vocals, too. Freddie Nagel's band presented **Ken Jackson** and **Bob Locken** as vocalists. In the late 1940's **Paul Neighbors** did his own vocals with help from **Ralph Anthony.** George Olsen's 1924 Orchestra featured **Billy Murray, Jack Gifford, Jerry Baker, Bob Borger** and **Bob Rice.** Leader **Will Osborne** was known to do his own vocals.

You will recall the popular singing group **6 Hits** and a Miss: **Bill Seckler, Tony Paris, Marvin Bailey, Lee Gotch, Vincent Degen,** and **Mac McLean** are the **6 Hits** who performed for Capitol Records and on **Bob Hope's** show and backed **Dick Haymes** on some Decca discs. **Gene Howard** began his career in Nashville with Bob Chester's boys. With Stan Kenton by age 21, **Gene** shared the bandstand with absolute Song Stars Anita O'Day and June Christy.

Larry Dean sang with Jimmy Palmer's band, **Allan King** and **Kenny Kennistan** with Bill Pannell. **Tony Pastor** did the honors himself in his famous band that featured him singing *Movie Tonight,* a charming duet with Song Star Rosemary Clooney. Besides **Mel Tormé,**

Ben Pollack spawned lots of male vocalists: **Frank Silvano, Frank Bauer, Dick Robertson, Jim Hardy,** and **Scrappy Lambert.** Teddy Powell's band starred **Gene Barry** (later, an actor), and **Skip Nelson** (mentioned earlier). **Louis Prima** was a terrific singer in his own band (How about that *Old Black Magic* with Keely Smith), just as **Carl Ravazza** sang in his own band. **Eddie Ryan** vocalized with Barney Rapp, with whom Doris Day got her start.

NBC music king Leo Reisman had **Lee Sullivan** and **Larry Stewart** as boy singers besides others mentioned here. **Ralph Young** graced Tommy Reynolds' bandstand, and **Eddie Farley, Vic Engle,** and **Wayne Gregg** did the honors in **Mike Riley's** New York band, as did **Mike** himself. **Buddy Rogers** was another singing bandleader with help from **Jack Douglas** and **Bob Hannon.** Jan Savitt's Philadelphia band presented **Bon Bon** (actually **George Tunnell**—remember his great version of *720 In the Books?*), **Joe Martin, and Bob D'Andrea. Jimmy Saunders, Tommy Leonetti, Tommy Mercer,** and **Gary Stevens** all sang with Charlie Spivak's big band. A proud product of Philadelphia like our **Lou Lanza, Jimmy Saunders** was rated one of the best singers of the era by *Downbeat Magazine*. His Charlie Spivak recordings *Lucky Old Sun* and *You Belong to My Heart* were hits. He also recorded the tune *One Dozen Roses* while with Harry James.

Dick Stabile featured **Jimmie Palmer** and **Bert Shaw** in his band. **Blue Steele's** Atlanta, Georgia, band featured **Blue Steele** himself as well as **Bob Nolan** and **George Marks. Dick Harding** and **Buddy Stewart** sang with Claude Thornhill, and **Al Trace** showcased himself on numbers like *You Call Everybody Darling* and the silly *Mairzy Doats,* while **Orrin Tucker** featured himself, along with **Jack Bartell** and **Eddie Rice. Ray Hawkins** and **Don Brown** were the singers with Tommy Tucker. **Tom Waring** sang with brother Fred Waring and his great band along with **Frank Sylvano.**

Ted Weems spawned **Perry Como, Dusty Rhodes, Country Washbourne, Parker Gibbs,** and **Wes Vaughn** as his band singers. **Gordon Maile, Frankie Sanders, Walter Bloom, Jules Herman, Bob Paige,** all graced Lawrence Welk's bandstand. Paul Whiteman's King of Jazz Orchestra featured **The Rhythm Boys** with **you know who, Al Rinker,** and **Harry Barris.** Others were **Charles Gaylord, Austin Young, Red Mac Kensie, Bob Lawrence, Jack Fulton, Ken Darby,** and a kid named **Johnny Mercer. The Hi-Lo's, Clark Burroughs, Bob Morse, Gene Puerling,** and **Dan Shelton** sang some beautiful close harmony pieces, as did the **Mel-Tones,** covered in **Mel Tormé's** chapter.

King Pleasure was **Clarence Beeks** whose first claim to fame was his version of *I'm In The Mood for Love* on Prestige Records. **Alan Dale** was one of the trio with **Don Cornell** and **Johnny Desmond** on the popular recording *Heart of My Heart.* Don't forget his version of *Cherry Pink and Apple Blossom White.* And, do you remember vocalist **Don Cherry's** *Thinking of You?* I do!

David Allyn and **Bob Manning** both are fine baritones in the style of **Dick Haymes.** Bob's *The Nearness of You* rivals the best of them. **Allyn** was more jazz than romantic ballad. His version of Berlin's little-known *Blue Echoes* is just great listening. **Skinnay Ennis,** a band leader and band singer who favored us with *Got a Date With An Angel*—also his band's theme, played a lot on **Bob Hope's** shows. By the way, **Bob Hope** was a band singer of sorts, especially with Les Brown's Band. He sang with **Bing** in the seven "Road" films and in his own films, and how about his evergreen theme on the recording with Shirley Ross—*Thanks For the Memory* from the film *The Big Broadcast of 1938.* It still works.

Mark Murphy is a cool jazz vocalist of the **Mel Tormé** school and is still at it today with a great following, as was sometime singer **Chet Baker,** who also played a lot of jazz trumpet in the fifties. Got to mention contemporary vocalist/pianist **Michael Feinstein** who sings great Gershwin and mostly classic pop in New York cabarets today. **Bobby Short** is a longtime player in this arena and is much revered as the quintessential cabaret singer. **Tom Postilio** needs note here too, although he was featured in my book *The Best Damn Trumpet Player* last year. His recent appearance in the Oak Room of the Algonquin Hotel is now legendary.

Jimmy Durante, once a ragtime pianist in a New Orleans jazz band, recorded with studio bands, played with Matty Malneck's Octet, sang in countless movies and on television. *Inka Dinka Doo,* from the film *Palooka,* was his long time theme. Jimmy was always helping other singers find their way into the big-time. He encouraged my friend **Don Cornell** early in his career.

Lou Monte used to sing live on WAAT, New Jersey. Winning two gold records for his *Pepino, the Italian Mouse,* both single and album (a

**"Ya gotta start each day off wid a song" the one and only Jimmy Durante.
Saved this photo from my old NBC, Colgate Comedy Hour Days.
(Richard Grudens Collection)**

million seller in 1962), Lou was only the second perfomer on Frank
Sinatra's fledgling Reprise Records. Sinatra was the first. Lou's recordings *I Really Don't Want to Know* and *She's An Old Fashioned Girl* are
two of his best. It proved that Lou was not just a great Italian singer. I
always liked his rendition of *I Have An Angel In Heaven.* We lost Lou in
1989.

That Ol' Black Magic was sung by the great night club performer
Billy Daniels (it became his theme), who started singing with Erskine
Hawkins in 1934 at Alabama State College and also recorded with **Fats
Waller.** He appeared on Broadway in both *Golden Boy* with **Sammy
Davis, Jr.,** *Hello Dolly* with Pearl Bailey, *Bubbling Brown Sugar* (in
London), and made a feature film with my friend **Frankie Laine.**

Al Bowlly was a prolific English recording artist of the '20s and
'30s. He sang with Ray Noble and Victor Young's orchestras in New

York making a great American impression after years of recording in Europe.

Some other groups were **The Four Aces** (*Love is a Many Splendored Thing*), **The Four Lads** (*Moments to Remember*), **The Lettermen, The Hi-Lo's, The Four Freshmen, The Ames Brothers** (*You, You, You*), and the lone **Roy Kral** (half of the **Jackie(Cain)** and **Roy** team), contributing their versions of the songs of the era.

Bill Hayes who sang with Godfrey, and later on Broadway in a Richard Rodgers musical *Me and Juliet* singing *The Big Black Giant* is a voice I still enjoy.

Engelbert Humperdinck (*Release Me*) and **Tom Jones** (*I'll Never Fall in Love Again*) are out-of-era singing favorites of millions who cannot go unmentioned in any book of singers.

The great French entertainer and singer **Maurice Chevalier,** requires a book for his career alone. (It's been written) His masterpiece *Mimi* was my favorite, as was *Thank Heaven For Little Girls* from the film *Gigi*.

The Ames Brothers (Richard Grudens Collection)

ROBERTO TIRADO—Walking in Sergio Franchi's shoes.

Once upon a time on Long Island, a veteran television anchor weatherman named **Roberto Tirado** developed a great following and appeared at community charity events as a singer. Yes, a singer. Then, during an appearance at The Tilles Center, Long Island's Carnegie Hall, entertainer Steve Allen caught **Roberto's** performance and inquired: "Was that *you* who created the screaming I just heard backstage? Well, it was a pleasure to hear you sing so well."

That did it! With that kind of encouragement, Roberto's singing career surfaced and he promptly recorded a great CD titled *Prisoner of Love*. This writer, actor, producer, and Emmy-winning weatherman, can really sing. Sounding a little bit like **Billy Eckstine** and **Dick Haymes** on one single track alone, Roberto also rises to dramatic heights with the selections *Begin the Beguine* and Cole Porter's great standard *Night and Day*. And, a credit to his Latino heritage, **Roberto** sings *Besame Mucho*, reflecting his feel and intense passion for lyrics. "Like Sinatra, I truly believe the words of a song." He acts out the lyric. He emotionalizes every note. He entertains while he sings.

A devotee of singer **Sergio Franchi:** "It made me sad to realize that an Italian romantic tenor of **Sergio's** stature would no longer grace the stages of America," he said.

Roberto explained to me that his quest is to preserve **Sergio Franchi's** memory, and, after meeting with and singing for Franchi's wife, Eva, she has agreed to allow **Roberto** to sing many of **Sergio's** arrangements. "My dream is to perform his songs—and to try to do justice to this great singer's memory," **Roberto** said.

Roberto is currently talking with the great record producer Ettore Stratta about recording some of the great Italian songs with the London Symphony. Keep tuned, America.

And, last, but nevertheless wonderful, is **Mose Allison,** who lives in the same town on Long Island as I do. A songwriter and piano-playing vocalist like **Nat Cole, Mose** has produced over 30 albums. He sings mostly ethnic music, as he was influenced by **Louis Armstrong** and **Fats Waller,** who were his father's favorites. He phrases like **Nat Cole** and infuses humor into his early songs as **Louis Jordan** used to. **Mose** played piano in the Old Miss Dance Band at the University of Mississippi. With wry lyrics and a special brand of New Orleans-style jazz—

219

if you will—his songs reflect the human condition delivered in an intelligent, but dry, conversational style. In Smithtown, Long Island, he and his wife Audre, a retired school teacher, have raised four children, including Amy, who has followed in her dad's footsteps, except in country music style. We love Irving Berlin and Cole Porter, but **Mose Allison** sings his own songs: *Hello Universe, Was,* and his most popular tune *Parchman Farm,* now considered a blues standard.

Roberto Tirado smiles for my cameraman. (Richard Grudens Collection)

BIBLIOGRAPHY

Crosby, Bing, with Pete Martin. *Call Me Lucky.* New York: Simon and Schuster, 1953.

Dooner, Roger, and Maurice Dunn. *Dick Haymes Society Newsletters.* Birmingham, England, and Minneapolis, Minn: Dick Haymes Society, Various Dates.

Ellington, Edward Kennedy. *Music is My Mistress.* New York: Doubleday & Co., 1973.

Erlewine, Michael, Editor. *All Music Guide to Jazz.* San Francisco, Cal.: 1996.

Feather, Leonard, and Ira Gitler. *The Encyclopedia of Jazz.* New York: Horizon Press, 1976.

Fisher, Eddie. *Eddie: My Life, My Loves.* New York: Harper & Row, 1981.

Friedwald, Will. *Jazz Singing.* New York: Macmillan Publishing, 1990-92.

Hall, Fred. *Diagogues In Swing.* Ventura, Ca.: Pathfinder Publishing, 1989.

Hall, Fred. *More Dialogues In Swing.* Ventura, Ca.: Pathfinder Publishing, 1991.

Harris, Jay S. *TV Guide: The First 25 Years.* New York: Simon and Schuster, 1978.

Haskins, Jim. *The Cotton Club.* New York: Hippocrene Books, 1977.

Hope, Bob, and Pete Martin. *The Last Christmas Show.* New York: Doubleday & Co., 1974.

Hope, Bob, and William Robert Faith. *A Life In Comedy.* New York: G.P. Putnam's Sons, 1982.

Jablonski, Edward. *Harold Arlen: Happy with the Blues.* New York: A Da Capo Press, 1986.

Kennedy, Don, and Hagan Williams. *Big Band Jump Newsletter.* Atlanta, Ga: Various Dates.

Laine, Frankie, and Joseph F. Laredo. *That Lucky Old Sun.* Ventura, Cal: Pathfinder Publishing, 1993.

Lees, Gene. *Singers and the Song.* New York: Oxford University Press, 1987.

Oberfirst, Robert. *Al Jolson: You Ain't Heard Nothin' Yet.* New York: A.S. Barnes & Co.,Inc., 1980.

Osterholm, J. Roger. *Bing Crosby: A Bio-Bibliography.* Westport, Conn.: Greenwood Press, 1994.

Palmer, Tony. *All You Need is Love: The Story of Popular Music.* New York: Grossman Publishers, 1976.

Pleasants, Henry. *The Great American Popular Singers*. New York: Simon and Schuster, 1974.

Rust, Brian. *The Complete Entertainment Discography*. New Rochelle, New York: Arlington House, 1973.

Settel, Irving. *A Pictorial History of Radio*. New Jersey, Castle Books, 1970.

Simon, George. *The Big Bands*. New York: Macmillan Publishing Co, 1967.

Simon, George. *Glenn Miller*. New York: Thomas Y. Crowell Co., 1974.

Tormé, Mel. *It Wasn't All Velvet*. New York: Viking Penquin, 1988.

Vallee, Rudy. *Kisses & Tells*. Canoga Park, Cal: Major Books, 1976.

Waller , Maurice, and Anthony Calabrese. *Fats Waller*. New York: Shirmer Books, 1977.

Walker, Leo. *Big Band Almanac*. Hollywood, Cal: Vinewood Enterprises, 1978.

Whiting, Margaret, and Will Holt. *It Might As Well Be Spring*. New York: William Morrow & Co, 1987.

WNEW. *Where the Melody Lingers On*. New York: Nightingale Gordon, 1984.

CELEBRITY PROFILES PUBLISHING
BOX 344 Main Street
STONYBROOK, NY 11790
(516) 862-8555 FAX 862-0139

The **BEST DAMN TRUMPET PLAYER**
ISBN 1-57579-011-4   196 Pages 55 Photos
Price $ 15.95

Please send_____copies.

****

The **SONG STARS**
ISBN 1-57579-045-9   240 Pages 60 Photos
Price $ 17.95

Please send_____copies.

****

The **MUSIC MEN**
ISBN 1-57579-097-1   248 Pages 77 Photos
PRICE $ 17.95

Please send_____copies.

****

NAME _____

ADDRESS _____

CITY, TOWN, STATE _____ZIP CODE _____

Include $ 3.00 for Priority Mail (2 days arrival time) for up to 2 books.

Enclose check or money order. Order will be shipped immediately.

For CREDIT CARDS, please fill out as shown below:

Card # _____Exp. Date _____

Signature _____

VISA___AMEX___DISCOVER___MASTER CARD___ (CHECK ONE)

223

Index

225

226

227

229

231